contents

STRIPED hoodie

SIZES
Sized for Child's 2, 4, 6, 8 and 10
Shown in size 4.

MEASUREMENTS
Chest (closed) 26 (29, 31½, 33, 34½)"/66 (73.5, 80, 83.5, 87.5)cm
Length 13¼ (14½, 16, 17¼, 18½)"/33.5 (37, 40.5, 44, 47)cm
Upper arm 12½ (13, 13½, 14, 14)"/31.5 (33, 34.5, 35.5, 35.5)cm

GAUGE
18 sts and 24 rows to 4"/10 cm over St st using size 8 (5mm) needles.
Take time to check gauge.

K3, P1 RIB
(multiple of 4 plus 3)
Row 1 (RS) K3, *p1, k3; rep from * to end.
Row 2 P3, *k1, p3; rep from * to end.
Rep rows 1 and 2 for k3, p1 rib.

STRIPE PATTERN
Work 8 rows MC, 8 rows CC.
Rep these 16 rows for stripe pattern.

BACK
With smaller needles and MC, cast on 55 (63, 67, 71, 75) sts. Work 8 rows in k3, p1 rib, inc 3 sts evenly over last (WS) row—58 (66, 70, 74, 78) sts.

Beg stripe pat
Change to larger needles and St st (k on RS, p on WS). Beg with a RS row, work 72 (80, 88, 96, 104) rows in stripe pat. Place 17 (21, 23, 24, 25) sts each end on holders for back shoulders, place center 24 (24, 24, 26, 28) sts on a 3rd holder for back neck.

MATERIALS
Yarn ④
• 7oz/200g, 310yd/290m (8¾oz/250g, 390yd/360m; 10½oz/300g, 470yd/430m; 10½oz/300g, 470yd/430m; 12¼oz/350g, 540yd/500m) of any worsted weight wool yarn each in jade green (MC) and aqua (CC)

Needles
• One pair each sizes 6 and 8 (4 and 5mm) needles *or size to obtain gauge*
• Three Size 8 (5.5mm) double-pointed needles (dpns) for 3-needle bind-off

Notions
• Size H/8 (5mm) crochet hook
• One red separating zipper
• Sewing needle and thread to match yarn.
• Stitch holders and stitch markers

RIGHT FRONT
With smaller needles and MC, cast on 28 (32, 36, 36, 36) sts.
Row 1 (RS) K1 (selvage st), work to end in k3, p1 rib.
Row 2 Work 31 sts in k3, p1 rib, k1 (selvage st). Rep last 2 rows 3 times more, inc 2 (2, 0, 1, 2) sts evenly over last (WS) row—30 (34, 36, 37, 38) sts.

Beg stripe pat
Change to larger needles.
Keeping first st in garter st (k every row), work in stripe pat in St st until piece measures 2"/5cm less than back, end with a WS row.

Shape neck
Next row (RS) Bind off 7 sts, work to end. Cont to shape neck as foll:
At neck edge, bind off 3 sts once, then dec 1 st at neck edge every other row 3 times—17 (21, 23, 24, 25) sts. Work even until piece is same length as back. Place sts on holder.

LEFT FRONT
With smaller needles and MC, cast on 28 (32, 36, 36, 36) sts.
Row 1 (RS) Work to last st in k3, p1 rib, k1 (selvage st).
Row 2 K1 (selvage st), work to end in k3, p1 rib. Work as for back, reversing shaping.

Shoulder seams
Note Seam will be visible on RS of garment.
Join shoulders using 3-needle bind-off as foll:
With WS facing tog, and front of garment facing you, place sts of back and front left shoulders on 2 dpns. With a 3rd dpn and MC, k first st from front needle tog with first st from back needle, *k next st from front and back needles tog, pass first st over 2nd st to bind off; rep from * until all sts are bound off. Cut yarn and fasten off. Rep for right shoulder.

SLEEVES
Place markers on front and back 6¼ (6½, 6¾, 7, 7)"/16 (16.5, 17, 18, 18) cm down from shoulder seams. With RS facing, larger needles and MC (CC, MC, CC, CC) pick up and k 56 (58, 60, 64, 64) sts between markers. Beg with row 9 (2, 13, 6, 1) work 48 (55, 61, 66, 72) rows in stripe pattern, and AT THE SAME TIME, dec 1 st each edge every 2nd (4th, 4th, 4th, 4th) row 7 (9, 9, 9, 6) times, then every 4th (6th, 6th, 6th, 6th) row 7 (3, 3, 4, 7) times—28 (34, 36, 38, 38) sts. Change to MC. K 1 row and dec 1 (3, 1, 3, 3) sts evenly across row—27

STRIPED hoodie

(31, 35, 35, 35) sts. Change to smaller needles. Beg with row 2, work 7 rows in k3, p1 rib. Bind off sts in rib.

FINISHING
Sew side and sleeve seams.

Hood
With RS facing, larger needles and MC (CC, MC, CC, MC) pick up and k 16 sts along right front neck edge, k 24 (24, 24, 26, 28) sts from back neck holder; pick up and k 16 sts along left front neck edge—56 (56, 56, 58, 60) sts. Beg with row 2, work in stripe pat as foll:
Next row (WS) P7 (7, 7, 8, 9), place marker (pm), *p14, pm; rep from * twice more, p to end.
Next (inc) row *K to marker, M1, sl marker; rep from * 3 times more, k to end. Rep inc row every other row 3 times more—72 (72, 72, 74, 76) sts. Cont even in stripe pat for 47 (55, 63, 71, 79) rows more. Divide sts in half and place on 2 dpns. Work 3-needle bind-off

as for shoulder seams. With crochet hook and MC, work 1 row sc around front edge of hood.

Right pocket
With larger needles and CC, cast on 18 sts. Working in stripe pat, work 2 rows even. Inc 1 st at end of next row, then every other row 3 times more—22 sts. Work 1 row even. Dec 1 st at end of next row, then every other row 10 times more—11 sts. Work 1 row even. Bind off. With crochet hook and MC, work 1 row sc along long slanted edge of pocket.

Left pocket
With larger needles and CC, cast on 18 sts. Work as for right pocket, reversing all shaping.
Place pockets on fronts above lower rib and 1 row outside of garter st edge. Leaving long slanted edges open, sew pockets to front.
Sew zipper in place. ■

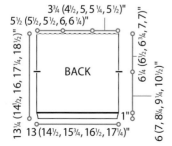

3¾ (4½, 5, 5 ¼, 5½)"
5½ (5½, 5½, 6, 6¼)"
13¼ (14½, 16, 17¼, 18½)"
BACK
6 ¼ (6½, 6¾, 7, 7)"
6 (7, 8¼, 9¼, 10½)"
1"
13 (14½, 15¾, 16½, 17¼)"

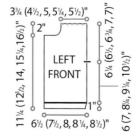

3¾ (4½, 5, 5 ¼, 5½)"
2"
11¼ (12½, 14, 15¼, 16½)"
LEFT FRONT
6 ¼ (6½, 6¾, 7, 7)"
6 (7, 8¼, 9¼, 10½)"
1"
6½ (7½, 8, 8¼, 8½)"

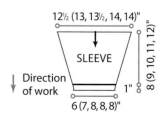

12½ (13, 13½, 14, 14)"
SLEEVE
Direction of work
8 (9, 10, 11, 12)"
1"
6 (7, 8, 8, 8)"

ZIPPERED pullover

SIZES
Sized for Child's 2, 4, 6, 8 and 10.
Shown in size 4.

MEASUREMENTS
Chest 26½ (29, 31, 33, 35)"/67.5 (73.5, 78.5, 83.5, 89)cm
Length 14 (15, 16, 18, 20)"/35.5 (38, 40.5, 45.5, 51)cm
Upper arm 12½ (13, 13½, 14, 14)"/31.5 (33, 34.5, 35.5, 35.5)cm

GAUGE
18 sts and 24 rows to 4"/10cm over St st using size 8 (5mm) needles.
Take time to check gauge.

BACK
With straight needles, cast on 60 (66, 70, 74, 78) sts. Beg with a RS row, work 8 rows in St st (k on RS, p on WS).
Next row (RS) P to end for turning ridge.
Next row Purl.
Cont in St st until piece measures 14 (15, 16, 18, 20)"/35.5 (38, 40.5, 45.5, 51)cm from turning ridge, end with a WS row.
Next row (RS) K18 (20, 22, 22, 23) and place sts on holder for right back shoulder, k24 (26, 26, 30, 32) and place sts on 2nd holder for back neck, k to end and place rem 18 (20, 22, 22, 23) sts on 3rd holder for left back shoulder.

FRONT
Work as for back until piece measures 7 (8, 9, 11, 13)"/17.5 (20, 22.5, 27.5, 33)cm from turning ridge, end with a WS row.

Divide for zipper placket
Next row (RS) K30 (33, 35, 37, 39), join 2nd ball of yarn, sl 1, k to end.
Next row (WS) P30 (33, 35, 37, 39) for right front, with first ball, sl 1, p to end.

MATERIALS
Yarn 4
• 12¼oz/350g, 540yd/500m (12¼oz/350g, 540yd/500m; 14oz/400g, 620yd/570m; 17½oz/500g, 770yd/710m; 19¼oz/550g, 850yd/780m) of any worsted weight wool yarn in aqua

Needles
• One pair size 8 (5mm) needles *or size to obtain gauge*
• Three size 8 (5mm) double-pointed needles (dpns)
• Size 8 (5mm) circular needle, 16"/40cm long

Notions
• Stitch holders and markers
• One 7"/18cm non-separating zipper from Coats & Clark, F72 Style 7", #4B pilot blue
• Sewing needle, thread and straight pins

Working both sides at the same time with separate balls of yarn, cont as established, slipping first st at placket edge every other row until piece measures 12 (13, 14, 16, 18)"/30.5 (33, 35.5, 40.5, 46)cm from turning ridge, end with a WS row.

Shape neck
Next row (RS) For left side, k to placket edge; for right side, bind off 6 (7, 7, 9, 10) sts, k to end.
Next row (WS) For left side, p24 (26, 28, 28, 29); for right side, bind off 6 (7, 7, 9, 10) sts, k to end.
Working both sides at the same time with separate balls of yarn, cont to bind off from each neck edge 2 sts twice, then dec 1 st every RS row 2 times. Work even on rem 18 (20, 22, 22, 23) sts each side until front is same length as back. Leave sts on needle.

Join shoulder seams
With WS facing each other, and front of sweater facing you, place sts of back and front right shoulders on two parallel dpns. Seam will be visible on RS of sweater. Work 3-needle bind-off as foll:

ZIPPERED pullover

With a 3rd dpn, k first st from front needle tog with first st from back needle, *k next st from front and back needles tog, slip first st over 2nd st to bind off; rep from * until all sts are bound off. Cut yarn and pull end through loop. Rep for left side.

SLEEVES

Place markers on front and back 6¼ (6½, 6¾, 7, 7)"/16 (16.5, 17, 18, 18)cm down from shoulder seams. With RS facing and straight needles, pick up and k 58 (60, 62, 64, 64) sts between markers. Work in St st, dec 1 st each side every 4th (6th, 6th, 6th, 6th) row 13 (2, 4, 11, 14) times, then every 2nd (4th, 4th, 4th, 0) row 1 (12, 10, 3, 0) times—30 (32, 34, 36, 36) sts. Work even until sleeve measures 11 (12, 13, 14, 15)"/28 (30.5, 33, 35.5, 38)cm, end with a WS row. P next row on RS for turning ridge. P next row. Cont in St st for 7 rows more. Bind off all sts.

FINISHING

Sew side and sleeve seams. Turn hems at bottom edge and cuffs to WS at turning ridge, and sew in place.

Collar

With RS facing and circular needle, beg at right front neck edge, pick up and k 16 (17, 17, 19, 20) sts along front right neck edge, k 24 (26, 26, 30, 32) sts from back holder, pick up and k 16 (17, 17, 19, 20) sts along front left neck edge—56 (60, 60, 68, 72) sts.

Row 1 (WS) Sl 1, p1, *k1, p1; rep from * to end.

Row 2 (RS) Sl 1, k the knit sts and p the purl sts. Rep row 2 until collar measures 2"/5cm. Bind off loosely and evenly in rib. Sew in zipper to placket edge. ∎

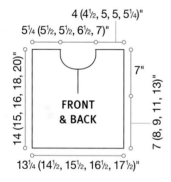

4 (4½, 5, 5, 5¼)"

5¼ (5½, 5½, 6½, 7)"

14 (15, 16, 18, 20)"

7"

FRONT & BACK

7 (8, 9, 11, 13)"

13¼ (14½, 15½, 16½, 17½)"

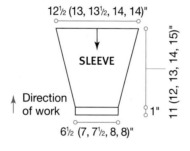

12½ (13, 13½, 14, 14)"

SLEEVE

11 (12, 13, 14, 15)"

↑ Direction of work

1"

6½ (7, 7½, 8, 8)"

NECKTIE
vest

SIZES
Sized for Child's 4 and 6. Shown in size 4.

MEASUREMENTS
Chest 28 (30)"/71 (76)cm
Length 15½ (16½)"/39.5 (42)cm

GAUGE
19 sts and 26 rows to 4"/10cm over St st using size 7 (4.5mm) needles.
Take time to check gauge.

K1, P1 RIB
(over an even number of sts)
Row 1 (RS) *K1, p1; rep from * to end.
Row 2 K the knit sts and p the purl sts.
Rep row 2 for k1, p1 rib.

NOTE
When changing colors, twist yarns on WS to prevent holes in work.

BACK
With MC, cast on 66 (72) sts. Work in k1, p1 rib for 6 rows, end with a WS row. Beg with a knit (RS) row, work even in St st until piece measures 8 (8½)"/20.5 (21.5)cm from beg, end with a WS row.

Armhole shaping
Bind off 4 sts at beg of next 2 rows. Dec 1 st at each end of next row, then every other row 2 times more—52 (58) sts. Work even until armhole measures 6½ (7)"/16.5 (18)cm, end with a WS row.

Shoulder shaping
Bind off 5 (6) sts at beg of next 2 rows, 4 (5) sts at beg of next 4 rows—26 sts. Place rem sts on holder for back neck.

MATERIALS
Yarn ④
Any worsted weight wool yarn
• 7oz/200g, 440yd/410m (10½oz/300g, 660yd/610m) in blue (MC)
• 3½oz/100g, 220yd/210m in orange (A) and green (B)
Needles
• One pair size 7 (4.5mm) needles *or size to obtain gauge*
• One size 7 (4.5mm) circular needle, 16"/40cm long
Notions
• Stitch holders
• Stitch markers
• Tapestry needle

FRONT
With MC, cast on 66 (72) sts. Work in k1, p1 rib for 6 rows, end with a WS row. Beg with a knit (RS) row, work 4 (10) rows in St st, end with a WS row. Place markers (pm) to mark center 26 sts.

Place chart
Next row (RS) K to marker, sl marker (sm), work row 1 of chart over next 26 sts, sm, k to end.
Cont in St st and foll chart in this manner, AT THE SAME TIME, when piece measures same as back to armhole, shape armholes same as for back—52 (58) sts. Work even through row 68 of chart. Armhole measures 4 (4½)"/10 (11.5)cm.

Neck and shoulder shaping
Next row (RS) Cont to foll chart as established, work to marker, sm, k6, join a 2nd ball of yarn and bind off center 14 sts, work to end of row.
Working both sides at once, dec 1 st from each neck edge every row 6 times—13 (16) sts. AT THE SAME TIME,

when all rows of chart are complete, cont in MC only. Work even until piece measures same as back to shoulder. Shape shoulders same as for back.

FINISHING
Block pieces to finished measurements. With tapestry needle and MC, embroider outline where indicated on chart. Sew shoulder and side seams.

Neckband
With circular needle, RS facing and A, k 26 sts from holder, pick up and k 48 (52) evenly around neck opening—74 (78) sts. Join, and pm for beg of rnd. Work 6 rnds in k1, p1 rib. Bind off all sts loosely in rib.

Armbands
With circular needle, RS facing and MC, pick up and k 68 (74) sts evenly around armhole opening. Join, and pm for beg of rnd. Work 4 rnds in k1, p1 rib. Bind off all sts loosely in rib. ■

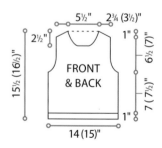

FRONT & BACK
5½" 2¾ (3½)"
2½" 1"
15½ (16½)" 6½ (7)"
7 (7½)"
1"
1"
14 (15)"

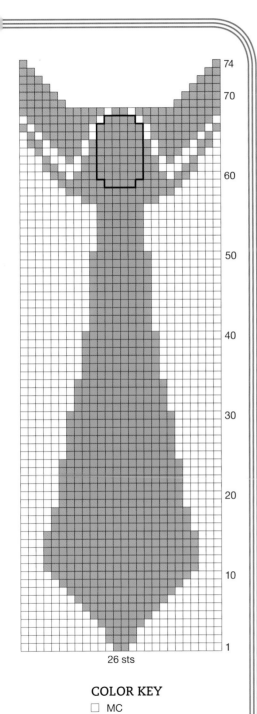

74
70

60

50

40

30

20

10

1

26 sts

COLOR KEY

☐ MC

▨ A

▨ B

⬚ outline st
with MC

KID'S STRIPED pullover

SIZES
Sized for Child's 2, 4, 6, 8, 10. Shown in size 2.

MEASUREMENTS
Chest 26 (28, 30, 32, 33)"/66 (71, 76, 81, 83.5)cm
Length 16 (17,18, 20, 22)"/40.5 (43, 45.5, 51, 56)cm
Upper arm 9¼ (10, 10, 10½, 11)"/23.5 (25.5, 25.5, 26.5, 28)cm

GAUGE
18 sts and 25 rows to 4"/10cm over St st using size 8 (5mm) needles.
Take time to check gauge.

STITCH GLOSSARY
Stripe pat for body
With A Work in St st for 6"/15cm.
With B Work in rev St st for 3"/7.5cm.
With C Work in St st for 3"/7.5cm.
With D Work in rev St st to end.

Stripe pat for sleeves
With A Work in St st for 7 (8½, 8½, 8, 7½)"/17.5 (21.5, 21.5, 20.5, 19)cm.
With B Work in rev St st for 3"/7.5cm.
With C Work in St st for 3"/7.5cm.
With D Work in rev St st to end.

NOTE
When changing from St st (k on RS, p on WS) to rev St st (p on RS, k on WS), k 1 row in new color on RS.

BACK
With A, cast on 58 (64, 68, 72, 74) sts. Work in stripe pat for body for 9¾ (10¼, 11, 12½, 14)"/24.5 (26, 28, 32, 35.5)cm, end with a WS row.

Shape armhole
Bind off 4 sts at beg of next 2 rows, 0 (2, 2, 2, 2) sts at beg of next 2 rows. Dec 1

MATERIALS
Yarn (4)
Any worsted weight wool yarn
• 3½oz/100g, 190yd/180m (5¼oz/150g, 290yd/270m; 5¼oz/150g, 290yd/270m; 7oz/200g, 380yd/350m; 7oz/200g, 380yd/350m) each in grey heather (A), medium brown (B) and beige (C)
• 3½oz/100g, 190yd/180m (3½oz/100g, 190yd/180m; 3½oz/100g, 190yd/180m; 5¼oz/150g, 290yd/270m; 5¼oz/150g, 290yd/270m) in cream (D)

Needles
• One pair size 8 (5mm) needles *or size to obtain gauge*
• One size 8 (5mm) circular needle, 16"/40cm long

Notions
• Stitch markers and holders

st each side every other row 2 (1, 1, 1, 1) times—46 (50, 54, 58, 60) sts. Work even in stripe pat until armhole measures 6¼ (6¾, 7, 7½, 8)"/16 (17, 17.5, 19, 20.5)cm from beg, end with a WS row.

Shape shoulder
Bind off 12 (13, 15, 16, 16) sts at beg of next 2 rows. Place rem 22 (24, 24, 26, 28) sts on a holder for neck.

FRONT
Work as for back until piece measures 13½ (14½, 15½, 17½, 19½)"/34 (36.5, 39, 44.5, 49.5)cm from beg, end with a WS row.

Shape neck
Next row (RS) Work 19 (20, 22, 23, 23) sts, join 2nd ball of yarn and bind off center 8 (10, 10, 12, 14) sts, work to end. Working both sides at once, bind

off 3 sts from each neck edge once, 2 sts once. Dec 1 st at each neck edge every other row 2 times. Work even until same length as back to shoulders. Bind off rem 12 (13, 15, 16, 16) sts each side for shoulders.

SLEEVES
With A, cast on 32 (32, 34, 34, 36) sts. Work in stripe pat for sleeves, AT THE SAME TIME, inc 1 st each side on row 11, then every 8th (8th, 12th, 10th, 10th) row 4 (5, 4, 6, 6) times more—42 (44, 44, 48, 50) sts. Work even in stripe pat until piece measures 10¾ (12¾, 13½, 14½, 15½)"/27.5 (32.5, 34.5, 37, 39.5)cm from beg, end with same stripe rows as on back to armhole.

Shape cap
Bind off 4 sts at beg of next 2 rows, bind off 0 (2, 2, 2, 2) sts at beg of next 2 rows. Dec 1 st each side on next row, then every 2nd row 12 (9, 8, 11, 11) times more, every 4th row 9 (2, 3, 2, 3) times—8 sts. Bind off.

FINISHING
Block pieces to measurements. Sew shoulder seams. Set in sleeves. Sew side and sleeve seams.

Neckband
With RS facing, circular needle and D, pick up and k 64 (68, 68, 72, 76) sts evenly around neck edge. Join and work in St st (k every rnd) or 1½"/4cm. Bind off loosely. ∎

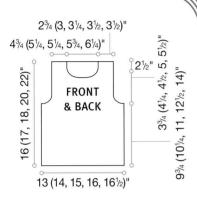

2¾ (3, 3¼, 3½, 3½)"

4¾ (5¼, 5¼, 5¾, 6¼)"

2½"

FRONT & BACK

16 (17, 18, 20, 22)"

3¾ (4¼, 4½, 5, 5½)"

9¾ (10¼, 11, 12½, 14)"

13 (14, 15, 16, 16½)"

9¼ (10, 10, 10½, 11)"

SLEEVE

4½ (5, 5¼, 5¾, 6½)"

10¾ (12¾, 13½, 14½, 15½)"

7 (7, 7½, 7½, 8)"

Paul Amato for Lvarepresents.com

11

BOY'S pullover

SIZES
Sized for Child's 2, 4, 6, 8. Shown in size 6.

MEASUREMENTS
Chest 24 (26, 28, 30)"/61 (66, 72, 76)cm
Length 12¾ (14¼, 15¾, 17¼)"/32.5 (36, 40, 44)cm
Upper arm 10 (10½, 11¼, 12)"/25.5 (26.5, 28.5, 30.5)cm

GAUGE
23 sts and 30 rows to 4"/10cm over wide rib pat using size 5 (3.75mm) needles.
Take time to check gauge.

K1, P1 RIB
(over an odd number of sts)
Row 1 (RS) *K1, p1; rep from * to last st, k1.
Row 2 K the knit sts and p the purl sts.
Rep row 2 for k1, p1 rib.

WIDE RIB PATTERN
(multiple of 6 sts plus 5)
Row 1 (RS) *K5, p1; rep from *, end k5.
Row 2 *P5, k1; rep from *, end p5.
Rep rows 1 and 2 for wide rib pat.

BACK
Cast on 71 (77, 83, 89) sts. Work in k1, p1 rib for 4 rows. Then work in wide rib pat until piece measures 7 (8, 9, 10)"/18 (20.5, 23, 25.5)cm from beg, end with a WS row.

Shape armhole
Bind off 4 (4, 5, 5) sts at beg of next 2 rows.
Next (dec) row (RS) P1, SKP, rib to last 3 sts, k2tog, p1.
Rep dec row every other row 2 (3, 3, 5) times more—57 (61, 65, 67) sts.

MATERIALS
Yarn ❸
• 7oz/200g, 460yd/430m (8¾oz/250g, 580yd/540m; 8¾oz/250g, 580yd/540m; 10½oz/300g, 690yd/640m) of any DK weight bamboo yarn in light blue

Needles
• One pair size 5 (3.75mm) needles *or size to obtain gauge*
• One size 5 (3.75mm) circular needle, 16"/40cm long

Notions
• Stitch holder or safety pin
• Stitch markers

Work even until armhole measures 5 (5½, 6, 6½)"/12.5 (14, 15, 16.5)cm, end with a WS row.

Shape shoulder
Bind off 5 (5, 5, 6) sts at beg of next 4 rows, 5 (6, 6, 5) sts at beg of next 2 rows. Bind off rem 27 (29, 33, 33) sts for back neck.

FRONT
Work as for back, including the armhole shaping, until armhole measures ½ (1, 1, 1½)"/1.5 (2.5, 2.5, 4)cm, end with a WS row.

Shape v-neck
Next row (RS) Cont to work the armhole shaping, work to center st, place center st on a st holder, join a 2nd ball of yarn and work to end.
Cont to work both sides at once and shape the v-neck as foll:
Dec row 1 (WS) Rib to last 3 sts of first side, p2tog tbl, k1; on 2nd side, k1, p2tog, rib to end.

Dec row 2 (RS) Work to last 3 sts of first side, k2tog, p1; on 2nd side, p1, SKP, work to end.
Rep last 2 dec rows 4 times more. Then work dec row 2 only 3 (4, 6, 6) times (with WS rows worked even)—15 (16, 16, 17) sts each side. Work even until armhole measures same as back.

Shape shoulder
Bind off from each shoulder edge 5 (5, 5, 6) sts twice, 5 (6, 6, 5) sts once.

SLEEVES
Cast on 41 (43, 45, 45) sts. Work in k1, p1 rib for 5 rows.
Next row (WS) P1, k1, p3 (4, 5, 5), *k1, p5; rep from *, end k1, p3 (4, 5, 5), k1, p1.
Next (inc) row (RS) K1, M1, work wide rib pat as established to last st, M1, k1.
Rep inc row (working inc'd sts into wide rib pat) every other row 9 (10, 11, 13) times more—59 (63, 67, 71) sts.
Work even until piece measures 3¼ (3½, 4, 4)"/8.5 (9, 10, 10)cm from beg, end with a WS row.

Shape cap
Bind off 4 (4, 5, 5) sts at beg of next 2 rows.
Dec row 1 (RS) P1, SKP, rib to last 3 sts, k2tog, k1.
Rep dec row 1 every other row 3 times more.
Dec row 2 (WS) K1, p2tog, rib to last 3 sts, p2tog tbl, k1.
Rep [dec rows 2 and 3] 4 (4, 3, 3) times, then rep dec row 1 every other row 4 (5, 7, 9) times. Bind off 2 sts at beg of next 4 rows. Bind off rem 9 (11, 13, 13) sts.

FINISHING
Block pieces lightly to measurements. Sew shoulder seams. Set in sleeves. Sew side and sleeve seams.

BOY'S pullover

Neckband

With RS facing and circular needle, pick up and k 27 (29, 33, 33) sts from back neck, 26 (26, 28, 28) sts from left neck edge, pm, pick up 1 st from center v-neck holder, 26 (26, 28, 28) sts from right front neck edge, pm to mark beg of rnd—80 (82, 90, 90) sts. Join to work in rnd.

Rnd 1 *K1, p1; rep from * for k1, p1 rib to 1 st before center marked st, S2KP, work in k1, p1 rib to end.

Rnd 2 K the knit sts and p the purl sts. Rep last 2 rnds for 1"/2.5cm, end with rnd 1.

Collar

Next rnd Rib to 12 sts before center marked st, bind off next 25 sts in rib, work in rib to end, turn.

Cont to work collar back and forth in rows.

Next row (WS) Work even.

Next row (RS) Work 3 sts, M1, work to last 3 sts, M1, rib 3.

Rep last 2 rows until collar measures 2½ (2½, 3, 3)"/6.5 (6.5, 7.5, 7.5)cm. Bind off loosely in rib. ■

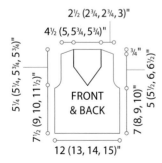

2½ (2¾, 2¾, 3)"

4½ (5, 5¾, 5¾)"

5¼ (5¼, 5¾, 5¾)"

¾"

FRONT & BACK

7½ (9, 10, 11½)"

7 (8, 9, 10)"

5 (5½, 6, 6½)"

12 (13, 14, 15)"

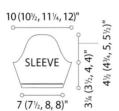

10 (10½, 11¼, 12)"

SLEEVE

3¼ (3½, 4, 4)"

4½ (4¾, 5, 5½)"

7 (7½, 8, 8)"

RACCOON hat

SIZE
Sized for child.

MEASUREMENTS
Circumference 18"/45.5cm

GAUGE
20 sts and 28 rows to 4"/10cm over St st using larger needles.
Take time to check gauge.

K1, P1 RIB
(over an odd number of sts)
Row 1 (RS) *K1, p1; rep from * to last st, k1.
Row 2 K the knit sts and p the purl sts. Rep row 2 for k1, p1 rib.

NOTE
When changing colors, twist yarns on WS to prevent holes in work.

HAT
With smaller needles and A, cast on 91 sts. Work in k1, p1 rib for 8 rows. Change to larger needles and B, work 4 row stripes, alternating B and A, in St st (k on RS, p on WS). AT THE SAME TIME when hat measures approx 5"/12.5cm from beg, ending with a WS row, begin to shape crown.

Shape crown
Next (dec) row (RS) [K11, k2tog] 7 times—84 sts. P 1 row.
Next (dec) row [K10, k2tog] 7 times—77 sts. P 1 row.
Next (dec) row [K9, k2tog] 7 times—70 sts.
Work in stripe pat and cont to dec in this way, with one less st before each k2tog, on every RS row, until 28 sts remain. P 1 row.
Next row [K2tog] 14 times.

MATERIALS

Yarn (4)
• 1¾oz/50g, 140yd/130m of any worsted weight wool yarn each in brown (A) and black (B)

Needles
• One pair each size 5 and 7 (3.75 and 4.5mm) needles
or size to obtain gauge

Notions
• Polyester stuffing
• Black thread
• Embroidery needle

Cut yarn, leaving long strand for sewing. Draw strand through rem 14 sts, tack tightly and sew back seam.

TAIL
With larger needles and B, cast on 28 sts. Work in St st and 4 row stripes, alternating B and A, for 7"/18cm.
Next (dec) row [K5, k2tog] 4 times—24 sts. P 1 row.

Cont to dec in this way, with one less st before each k2tog, on every RS row, until 16 sts rem.
Next row [K2tog] 8 times—8 sts.
Cut yarn, leaving long strand for sewing. Draw strand through rem 4 sts and tack tightly. Sew back seam, stuffing tail as you go. Attach to hat at back seam at top of first black stripe. ∎

RACCOON scarf

SIZE
Sized for child.

MEASUREMENTS
Tip to paw 4 x 42"/10 x 106.5cm

GAUGES
- 20 sts and 28 rows to 4"/10cm over St st using larger needles.
- 22 sts and 34 rows to 4"/10cm over garter st using larger needles.

Take time to check gauges.

NOTE
When changing colors, twist yarns on WS to prevent holes in work.

SCARF
With larger needles and C, cast on 4 sts.
*K 1 row.
Next (inc) row K1, M1, k to last st, M1, k1. Rep from * until 22 sts are on needle. Work even in garter st (k every row) until piece measures 3"/7.5cm from beg.

Mask
Note Wind two 60"/152.5cm strands of B from the skein to use for working the mask intarsia style.
Next row (RS) Join B (the skein) and work as foll: K3 B, k16 C, join one strand of B, k3 B.
Next row K3 B, k16 C, k3 B.
Next 2 rows K5 B, k12 C, k5 B.
Cont as established, using C and B and knitting 2 more sts with B on each side and 2 fewer sts with C in the center, on every RS row, until all 22 sts are being worked in B. Cut C and k 8 rows with B.
Next row (RS) K9 B, join A, k4 A, join second strand of B, k9 B.
Next row K9 B, k4 A, k9 B.
Cont working in B and A, knitting 2

fewer sts of B on each side and 4 more sts of A in the center, every RS row, until all 22 sts are being worked in A. Cut B and cont with A until piece measures approx 39"/99cm from beg, end with a WS row.

Legs
Next row (RS) K7, join 2nd ball of A and bind off center 8 sts, k to end. Work each leg separately for 2½"/6.5cm. Join B to each leg and k 7 rows. Bind off each side.

FINISHING
Tail
With larger needles and B, cast on 21 sts. Work in St st and 4 row stripes of B and A for 4½"/11.5cm, end with a WS row.
Next row *K5, k2tog; rep from * 3 times more—15 sts. P1 row.
Next (RS) row Cont to dec with 1 less st before each k2tog, on every RS row until 12 sts rem.
Next (RS) row [K2tog] 6 times—6 sts. Cut yarn, leaving long strand, draw through rem sts, tack tightly and sew back seam, stuffing tail as you go.

MATERIALS
Yarn 🔴4
Any worsted weight wool yarn
- 3½oz/100g, 280yd/260m in brown (A)
- 1¾oz/50g, 140yd/130m each in black (B) and cream (C)

Needles
- One pair each size 5 (3.75mm) and 7 (4.5mm) needles *or size to obtain gauges*

Notions
- One size E/4 (3.5mm) crochet hook (for nose)
- Polyester stuffing
- 2 white ½"/1.5cm 4-hole buttons
- Black thread and embroidery needle

Attach to body approx. 1¾"/3.5cm above center edge between legs.

Ears
With larger needles and A, cast on 7 sts. Work 4 rows even in St st (k 1 row, p1 row).
Next (dec) row (RS) K2tog, k3, k2tog. Purl 1 row.
Next (dec) row (RS) K2tog, k1, k2tog—3 sts.
Cut yarn, leaving long strand, draw through rem sts and tack tightly. Sew top and bottom of each ear to face, using photo as guide.

Eyes
Using photo as guide, sew buttons to center of mask with black thread in "x" formation.

Nose
With crochet hook and strand of B, make a chain of 12 sts, twist into a spiral, and tack down at center of face approx 1"/2.5cm above lower edge. ■

COLOR-YOKE cardigan

SIZES
Sized for Child 2, 4, 6, 8, 10. Shown in size 6.

MEASUREMENTS
Chest 26 (28, 30, 32, 34)"/66 (71, 76, 81, 86.5)cm
Length 12½ (14, 15½, 17½, 19½)"/32 (35.5, 39.5, 44.5, 49.5)cm
Upper arm 10¼ (11, 12, 12¼, 13)"/26 (28, 30.5, 31, 33)cm

GAUGE
16 sts and 20 rows to 4"/10cm over St st using size 8 (5mm) needles.
Take time to check gauge.

STRIPE PATTERN
Rows 1 and 2 With B, k.
Row 3 With MC, p.
Rows 4 and 5 With A, k.
Row 6 With A, p.
Rows 7 and 9 With B, k.
Row 8 With B, p.
Rows 10 and 11 With MC, k.
Row 12 With MC, p.
Rep rows 1–12 for stripe pat.

BODY
With MC and circular needle, cast on 104 (112, 120, 128, 136) sts. Do not join. Work back and forth in rows. Work 8 rows in garter st (k every row), end with a WS row. Beg with a k (RS) row, work in St st (k on RS, p on WS) until piece measures 7 (8, 9, 10½, 12)"/18 (20.5, 23, 26.5, 30.5)cm from beg, end with a RS row.

Divide for fronts and back
Next row (WS) P29 (31, 33, 35, 37) sts, place last 6 sts on RH needle on scrap yarn for left underarm, p52 (56, 60, 64,

MATERIALS

Yarn (4)
Any worsted weight wool yarn
- 12¼oz/350g, 500yd/460m (12¼oz/350g, 500yd/460m; 14oz/400g, 570yd/530m; 14oz/400g, 570yd/530m; 15¾oz/450g, 640yd/590m) in navy (MC)
- 1¾oz/50g, 80yd/80m each in orange (A) and red (B)

Needles
- Size 8 (5mm) circular needle, 24"/60 long *or size to obtain gauge*
- One set (5) size 8 (5mm) double-pointed needles (dpns)

Notions
- Scrap yarn, stitch holders and stitch markers
- 7 (8, 9, 9, 10) ¾"/19mm buttons

68) sts, place last 6 sts on RH needle on scrap yarn for right underarm, p to end of row. Do not cut yarn. Set aside.

SLEEVE
With dpns and MC, cast on 25 (26, 26, 27, 28) sts. Divide sts evenly onto 4 dpns. Join, taking care not to twist sts. Place marker for beg of rnd and sl marker every rnd.
Work 8 rnds in garter st (k 1 rnd, p 1 rnd), end with a p rnd.
Work in St st (k every rnd), inc 1 st at each end of 4th and every foll 4th (5th, 4th, 5th, 4th) rnd 7 (8, 10, 10, 11) times—41 (44, 48, 49, 52) sts.
Work even until piece measures 8½ (10½, 11½, 12½, 14)"/21.5 (26.5, 29, 32, 35.5)cm from beg.
Next rnd K3, place last 6 sts on RH needle on scrap yarn for underarm, dropping st marker. Cut yarn leaving a

12"/30.5cm tail. Place rem 35 (38, 42, 43, 46) sts on st holder. Set aside.

YOKE
Joining row (RS) With circular needle and MC, k23 (25, 27, 29, 31) sts (right front), k35 (38, 42, 43, 46) sts from first sleeve, k46 (50, 54, 58, 62) sts (back) dec 1 (0, 1, 1, 0) st at center, k35 (38, 42, 43, 46) sts from second sleeve, k23 (25, 27, 29, 31) sts (left front)—161 (176, 191, 201, 216) sts.
Beg with a p (WS) row, work 5 (7, 9, 11, 13) rows in St st, end with a WS row.
Dec row 1 (RS) *K3, k2tog; rep from * to last st, k1—129 (141, 153, 161, 173) sts.

Beg stripe pat
Beg with row 1, work foll stripe pat until yoke measures 3 (3½, 4, 4½, 5)"/7.5 (9, 10, 11.5, 12.5)cm from joining row, end with a WS row.
Dec row 2 (RS) *Work 2 sts, dec 2 sts by k2tog or p2tog; rep from * to last st, work 1 st—97 (106, 115, 121, 130) sts.
Cont in stripe pat until yoke measures 4½ (5, 5½, 6, 6½)"/11.5 (12.5, 14, 15, 16.5)cm from joining row, end with a WS row.
Dec row 3 (RS) *Work 1 st, dec 2 sts by k2tog or p2tog; rep from * to last st, work 1 st—65 (71, 77, 81, 87) sts.
Cont in stripe pat until yoke measures 5 (5½, 6, 6½, 7)"/12.5 (14, 15, 16.5, 18)cm from joining row, end with a WS row.
Next row (RS) With MC, k.
Next row With MC, p.
Dec row 4 (RS) K0 (1, 0, 0, 1), *k2, k2tog; rep from * to last 1 (2, 1, 1, 2), k1 (2, 1, 1, 2)—49 (54, 58, 61, 66) sts.
Work 7 rows in garter st, end with a WS row. Bind off rem sts knitwise.

FINISHING
Block pieces to measurements. Graft underarm seams using Kitchener st.

COLOR-YOKE
cardigan

Buttonband

With RS facing and MC, pick up and k 64 (70, 78, 88, 96) sts evenly spaced along right front edge. K next 7 rows, end with RS facing. Bind off knitwise. Place markers for 7 (8, 9, 9, 10) buttons, with the first ½"/1cm from neck edge, the last ½"/1cm from lower edge and the rem spaced evenly between.

Buttonhole band

With RS facing and MC, pick up and k 64 (70, 78, 88, 96) sts evenly spaced along left front edge. K 3 rows. **Next (buttonhole) row (RS)** K, working buttonholes to correspond to button markers as foll: yo, k2tog. K 3 rows. Bind off all sts knitwise. Sew on buttons. ■

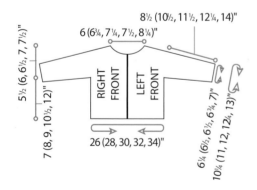

FROG sweater

SIZES
Sized for Child's 2, 4 and 6. Shown in size 2.

MEASUREMENTS
Chest 26½ (28, 30½)"/67.5 (71, 77.5)cm
Length 14½ (15½,16½)"/37 (39.5, 42)cm
Upper arm 11½ (12½, 13¼)"/29 (32, 33.5)cm

GAUGE
20 sts and 26 rows to 4"/10cm over St st using larger needles.
Take time to check gauge.

STRIPE PATTERN
Work in St st as foll: 4 rows B, 4 rows A. Rep the 8 rows for stripe pat.

NOTE
When changing colors, twist yarns on WS to prevent holes in work. Use a separate bobbin for each color section. Do not carry yarn across back of work.

BACK
With smaller needles and A, cast on 66 (70, 76) sts.
Row 1 (RS) *K1, p1; rep from * to end.
Row 2 (WS) *P1, k1; rep from * to end.
Rep rows 1 and 2 for k1, p1 rib 4 times more. Change to larger needles and work in St st (k on RS, p on WS) until piece measures 14½ (15½, 16½)"/37 (39.5, 42)cm from beg, end with RS row.
Next row (WS) Bind off 20 (21, 23) sts for right shoulder, work across 26 (28, 30) sts and place on holder. Bind off rem sts for left shoulder.

FRONT
Work same as for back until 6 (10, 14) rows of St st have been worked above rib.

MATERIALS
Yarn ③
Any DK weight wool blend yarn
- 8¾oz/250g, 390yd/360m (10½oz/300g, 470yd/430m; 12¼oz/350g, 540yd/500m) in blue (A)
- 3½oz/100g, 160yd/150m (5¼oz/150g, 240yd/220m; 5¼oz/150g, 240yd/220m) in green (B)
- 1¾oz/50g, 80yd/80m in brown (C)
- Small amounts in lime green (D) and in red (E)

Needles
- One pair each sizes 4 and 6 (3.5 and 4mm) needles
  or size to obtain gauge
- Two size 6 (4mm) double-pointed needles (dpns)
- One size 4 (3.5mm) circular needle, 16"/40cm long

Notions
- One size G/6 (4mm) crochet hook
- Embroidery needle
- Stitch marker

Beg chart
Next row (RS) With A, k31 (33, 36), join C and work 35 (37, 40) sts of chart pat. When 46 rows are complete, cont with A over all sts until piece measures 9¼ (10, 10¾)"/23.5 (25.5, 27)cm from beg, end with a WS row.

Shape v-neck
Next (dec) row (RS) K31 (33, 36), k2tog, join 2nd ball of yarn, ssk, k to end. Work 1 row even. Working both sides at once, dec 1 st at each neck edge every other row 10 (11, 12) times, then every 4th row twice—20 (21, 23) sts rem on each side. Work even until piece measures same as back to shoulders. Bind off.

SLEEVES
With smaller needles and A, cast on 34 (36, 36) sts. Work in k1, p1 rib for 10 rows. Change to larger needles.

Beg stripe pat
Next (inc) row (RS) Join B, k inc 4 (4, 6) sts evenly across—38 (40, 42) sts. Cont in St st and stripe pat, inc 1 st each side every 6th row 10 (11, 12) times—58 (62, 66) sts. Work even until piece measures 11½ (12½, 13½)"/29 (32, 34.5)cm from beg. Bind off.

FINISHING
Block pieces to measurements. Sew shoulder seams.

Neckband
With RS facing, circular needle and A, beg at right shoulder, k26 (28, 30) sts from holder, pick up and k 30 (32, 34) sts along left front neck, place marker (pm) for center of V-neck, pick up and k 30 (32, 34) sts along right front edge—86 (92, 98) sts. Join and pm for beg of rnd.

FROG
sweater

Next (dec) rnd *K1, p1; rep from * to 2 sts before center marker; k2tog, sl marker, ssk, *k1, p1; rep from * to end of rnd. Rep dec rnd every rnd 6 times more—72 (78, 84) sts. Bind off loosely. With center of bound-off sts of sleeve at shoulder seams, sew top of sleeve to front and back. Sew side and sleeve seams.

Eyes (make 2)

With smaller needles and D, cast on 5 sts. Make bobble as foll: Work in St st for 5 rows. Pass 4 sts, one at a time, over last st. Cut yarn leaving 8"/20.5cm tail from needle, thread through rem st. Thread needle with tail, and sew running st around outside of bobble. Pull up to shape and tack tightly. Attach as indicated on chart. With strand of C, put a st through center for eyeball.

Mouth

With embroidery needle and strand of B, sew chain stitch across mouth as indicated on chart.

Tongue

With crochet hook and strand of E, chain 8, join and stitch center tog. Attach end as indicated on chart.

Legs (make 2)

With 2 dpns and B cast on 6 sts. Work in I-cord as foll: *Knit one row. Without turning work, slide the sts back to beg of the row. Pull yarn tightly from the end of the row. Rep from * until I-cord is 5½"/14cm long. Cut yarn, thread through rem sts and pull tightly. Attach as indicated on chart, looping legs around and tacking down.

Grass

Cut ten 3½"/9cm strands of B. With crochet hook, holding 2 strands tog, attach as spot fringe on front as desired, or use photo as guide. ∎

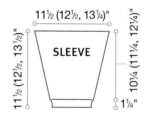

SLEEVE

11½ (12½, 13¼)"

11½ (12½, 13½)"

10¼ (11¼, 12¼)"

1¼"

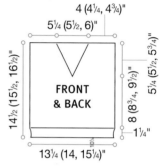

FRONT & BACK

4 (4¼, 4¾)"

5¼ (5½, 6)"

14½ (15½, 16½)"

8 (8¾, 9½)"

5¼ (5½, 5¾)"

1¼"

13¼ (14, 15¼)"

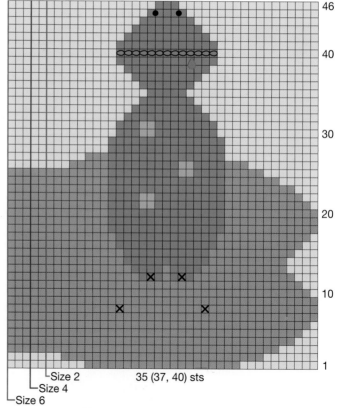

46

40

30

20

10

1

Size 2
Size 4
Size 6

35 (37, 40) sts

COLOR KEY

☐ Blue (A)
◼ Green (B)
▨ Brown (C)
▨ Lime Green (D)

🌢 tongue placement
⦿ eye placement
⊡ chain st embroidery
✖ leg placement

ROBOT mittens

SIZES
Sized for Child's 4, 6 and 8. Shown in size 4.

MEASUREMENTS
Length 6½ (7¼, 7¾)"/16.5 (18.5, 19.5)cm
Hand circumference 7"/18cm

GAUGE
16 sts and 24 rows to 4"/10cm over
St st using larger needles.
Take time to check gauge.

K1, P1 RIB
(over an even number of sts)
Row 1 *K1, p1; rep from * to end.
Row 2 K the knit sts and p the purl sts.
Rep row 2 for k1, p1 rib.

NOTES
1 When changing colors, twist yarns on
WS to prevent holes in work.
2 Use a separate bobbin for each color
section. Do not carry yarn across back
of work.

RIGHT MITTEN
With smaller needles and A, cast on 28
sts. Work in k1, p1 rib for 2 rows. Join B,
cont in rib for 2 rows. Rep last 4 rows,
then work 2 rows A once more. Change
to larger needles and join C. With C,
work 4 (6, 8) rows in St st (k on RS, p
on WS).

Beg thumb gusset
Next (inc) row (RS) K16, place marker
(pm), M1, k1, M1, pm, k to end—30 sts.
Next row (WS) Purl.

Beg chart
Next (inc) row (RS) K4, work 9-st chart
pat, k3, sl marker (sm), M1, k to marker,
M1, sm, k to end—32 sts.

MATERIALS
Yarn 4
• 3½oz/100g, 200yd/190m of any
worsted weight wool yarn each in
red (A), white (B), and black (C)
Needles
• One pair each sizes 5 and 7 (3.75
and 4.5mm) needles
or size to obtain gauge
Notions
• Two ⅜"/10mm white flat 4-hole
buttons
• Two ½"/12mm novelty buttons
• Sewing needle and black and white
thread
• Embroidery needle
• Stitch markers and stitch holders

Next row (WS) P, foll chart as established.
Rep last 2 rows twice more—36 sts.

Hand
Next row (RS) Work to marker, place 9
thumb sts on holder, M1, work to end—
28 sts. Cont to work chart pat through
row 18, then cont with C only until piece
measures 5½ (6¼, 6¾)"/14 (16, 17)cm
from beg, end with a WS row.

Shape top
Next (dec) row (RS) [K2, k2tog] 7
times—21 sts.
Next row (WS) Purl.
Next (dec) row (RS) [K1, k2tog] 7
times—14 sts.
Next row (WS) Purl.
Next (dec) row (RS) [K2tog] 7
times—7 sts.
Cut yarn and thread through rem sts,
leaving a long tail for sewing.

Thumb
Place 9 thumb sts on needle, rejoin C and
work as foll:

Row 1 (inc RS) K9, pick up and k 1 st
along thumb opening—10 sts.
Work even in St st until thumb measures
1½"/4cm, end with a WS row.
Next (dec) row (RS) [k2tog] 5 times—5
sts.
Cut yarn and thread through rem sts,
leaving a long tail for sewing.

LEFT MITTEN
Work same as for right mitten to thumb
gusset.

Beg thumb gusset
Next (inc) row (RS) K11, pm, M1, k1, M1,
pm, k to end—30 sts.
Next row (WS) Purl.

Beg chart
Next (inc) row (RS) K to marker, sm, M1,
k to marker, M1, sm, k3, work 9-st chart
pat, k4—32 sts.
Next row (WS) Purl, foll chart as
established.
Rep last 2 rows twice more—36 sts.

Hand
Next row (RS) Work to marker, M1,
place 9 thumb sts on holder, work to
end—28 sts.
Complete as for right mitten.

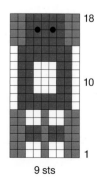

STITCH KEY
□ k on RS,
p on WS

⊙ eye
placement

COLOR KEY
■ red (A)
□ white (B)
■ black (C)

9 sts

FINISHING

Using tails, sew side and thumb seams. Using photo as guide, sew buttons in position for eyes with different colored thread. With strands of B, embroider antennae with chain st on top of robot head. ∎

ZIPPERED cardi

SIZES
Sized for Child's 2, 4, 6, 8, 10.
Shown in size 4.

MEASUREMENTS
Chest (closed) 27 (29, 31, 32½, 33¼)"/68.5 (73.5, 78.5, 82.5, 84.5)cm
Length 13 (15, 17, 19½, 20)"/33 (38, 43, 48, 51)cm
Upper arm 10 (11, 12, 13, 14)"/25.5 (28, 30.5, 33, 35.5)cm

GAUGE
20 sts and 26 rows to 4"/10cm over St st using larger needles.
Take time to check gauge.

K2, P2 RIB
(multiple of 4 sts, plus 2)
Row 1 *K2, p2; rep from *, end k2.
Row 2 K the knit sts and p the purl sts.
Rep row 2 for k2, p2 rib.

NOTE
Sweater is worked back and forth in one piece to the armholes.
Circular needle is used to accomodate large number of sts.

BODY
With smaller needle, cast on 134 (146, 154, 162, 166) sts. Work in k2, p2 rib for 3"/7.5cm.
Next row (RS) Change to larger needles, k34 (37, 39, 41, 42) for right front, pm, k66 (72, 76, 80, 82) for back, pm, k to end for left front. P one row.
Cont in St st (k on RS, p on WS) until piece measures 8 (9½, 11, 13, 13)"/20.5 (24, 28, 33, 33)cm from beg.

Shape armholes
Next row (RS) K to 5 sts before first marker, bind off next 10 sts, dropping marker, k to 5 sts before 2nd marker, bind off next 10 sts, dropping marker, k to end. Cont in St st on 29 (32, 34, 36, 37) sts of left front only, keeping back and right front sts on hold, until left front armhole measures 3½ (4, 4½, 5, 5½)"/9 (10, 11.5, 12.5, 14)cm.

Shape neck
Next row (WS) Bind off 5 (5, 6, 6, 7) sts, p to end. K 1 row.
Next row (WS) P1, p2tog, p to end. K 1 row. Rep last 2 rows 4 times more—19 (22, 23, 25, 25) sts.
Cont in St st until armhole measures 5 (5½, 6, 6½, 7)"/12.5 (14, 15, 16.5, 18)cm. Bind off all sts for shoulder.

RIGHT FRONT
Join yarn to right front and work to correspond to left front, reversing neck shaping by binding off at beg of RS rows and working decs as k1, ssk at beg of RS rows.

BACK
Join yarn to back and cont in St st on 56 (62, 66, 70, 72) sts until armhole measures 5 (5½, 6, 6½, 7)"/12.5 (14, 15, 16.5, 18)cm. Bind off.

SLEEVES
Note The sleeves are worked from top to cuff.
With larger needles, cast on 50 (56, 60, 64, 70) sts. Work 8 rows in St st.
Next (dec) row (RS) K1, ssk, k to last 3 sts, k2tog, k1. Cont in St st and rep dec row every 10th (10th, 8th, 10th 6th) row 3 (4, 6, 6, 9) times more—42 (46, 46, 50, 50) sts. Cont in St st until sleeve measures 7 (9, 10, 11, 12)"/18 (23, 25.5, 28, 30.5)cm from cast-on edge. Work in k2, p2 rib for 3"/7.5. Bind off loosely in rib.

FINISHING
Sew shoulder seams.

Collar
Beg at right front neck, with smaller needles and RS facing, pick up and k 38 (38, 46, 46, 46) sts evenly around neck. Work in garter st (knit every row) for 7 rows. Change to larger needles.
Next row (WS) K1 *inc 1 st in next st; rep from * to last st, k1—74 (74, 90, 90, 90) sts. Work in k2, p2 rib for 4½"/11.5cm. Bind off.

Edging
Beg at lower edge of left front, with size H/8 (5mm) crochet hook and RS facing, work backwards single crochet (working

MATERIALS
Yarn 4
• 10½oz/300g, 630yd/580m (10½oz/300g, 630yd/580m; 14oz/400g, 840yd/770m; 17½oz/500g, 1050yd/970m; 17½oz/500g, 1050yd/970m) of any worsted weight acrylic blend yarn in light green

Needles
• One each size 6 (4mm) and 8 (5mm) circular needle, 24"/60cm long *or size to obtain gauge*

Notions
• Size H/8 (5mm) crochet hook
• One separating zipper 12 (14, 16, 18, 18)"/30 (35, 40, 45, 45)cm from Coats & Clark F43, color #39B barberry red
• Stitch markers
• Sewing needle, thread and straight pins

ZIPPERED cardi

from left to right) into every other st along front edge to top of collar. Rep for right front, beg at top of collar and working to lower edge of ribbing.

Sew cast-on edge of sleeves to front and back armholes, sewing first 1"/2.5cm along 5 bound-off armhole sts. Sew sleeve seams. Sew zipper to front edges. ■

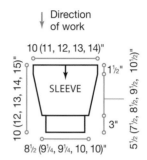

↓ Direction of work

10 (11, 12, 13, 14)"

SLEEVE

1½"

3"

10 (12, 13, 14, 15)"

5½ (7½, 8½, 9½, 10½)"

8½ (9¼, 9¼, 10, 10)"

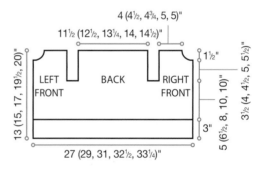

4 (4½, 4¾, 5, 5)"

11½ (12½, 13¼, 14, 14½)"

LEFT FRONT   BACK   RIGHT FRONT

1½"

13 (15, 17, 19½, 20)"

3½ (4, 4½, 5, 5½)"

5 (6½, 8, 10, 10)"

3"

27 (29, 31, 32½, 33¼)"

DOG MOTIF
pullovers

MATERIALS

Yarn

Any worsted weight wool and acrylic blend yarn

Checkerboard Dog
- 8¾oz/250g, 480yd/440m
(10½oz/300g, 570yd/430m;
10½oz/300g, 570yd/430m; 12¼oz/350g,
670yd/620m) in light brown (MC)
- 1¾oz/50g, 100yd/100m each in cream
(A), black (B) and red (C)

Dog with Scarf
- 8¾oz/250g, 480yd/440m
(10½oz/300g, 570yd/430m;
10½oz/300g, 570yd/430m; 12¼oz/350g,
670yd/620m) in slate blue (MC)
- 1¾oz/50g, 100yd/100m each in cream
(A), light brown (B) and red (C)
- Small amount in black for embroidery

Needles
- One pair each sizes 5 and 7 (3.75 and
4.5mm) needles *or size to obtain gauge*

SIZES
Sized for Child's 2 (4, 6, 8). Shown in size 2.

MEASUREMENTS
Chest 25 (27½, 30, 32)"/63.5 (69.5, 76, 81.5)cm
Length 13½ (15, 16, 17)"/34.5 (38, 40.5, 43)cm
Upper arm 11 (12, 13, 14)"/28 (30.5, 33, 35.5)cm

GAUGE
18 sts and 25 rows to 4"/10cm over St st using larger needles.
Take time to check gauge.

NOTES
1 Both sweaters are the same pattern but with different dog motifs knit in the center of the fronts.
2 Use a separate bobbin or length of yarn for each block of colors. When changing colors, twist yarns on WS to prevent holes in work.

K3, P2 RIBBING
(multiple of 5 sts plus 2)
Row 1 (RS) P2, *k3, p2; rep from * to end.
Row 2 K the knit sts and p the purl sts.
Rep row 2 for k3, p2 rib.

BACK
With smaller needles and MC, cast on 57 (62, 67, 72) sts. Work in k3, p2 rib for 6 rows, dec 1 (0, inc 1, 0) st at end of last row—56 (62, 68, 72) sts. Change to larger needles and work in St st until piece measures 8 (9, 9½, 10)"/20.5 (23, 24, 25.5)cm from beg.

Shape armhole
Bind off 4 (4, 5, 5) sts at beg of next 2 rows—48 (54, 58, 62) sts. Work even until armhole measures 5½ (6, 6½, 7)"/14 (15, 16.5, 17.5)cm. Bind off all sts.

DOG MOTIF pullovers

Work even until armhole measures same as back. Bind off rem 12 (14, 16, 17) sts each side for shoulders.

FRONT (DOG WITH SCARF)

Work as for back until 7 (9, 11, 13) rows of St st have been worked above rib.

Beg chart pat

Row 1 (RS) With MC, k3 (6, 9, 11), work row 1 of dog with scarf chart over next 52 sts, k to end with MC.
Cont in chart as established through row 57, AT THE SAME TIME, when same

length as back to armhole, shape armhole same as back. After all chart rows have been worked, cont with MC only until armhole measures 3½ (4, 4, 4½)"/9 (10, 10, 11.5)cm. Shape neck and complete as for checkerboard dog.

SLEEVES

With smaller needles and MC, cast on 27 (32, 32, 32) sts. Work in k3, p2 rib for 6 rows, inc 1 (dec 2, dec 2, 0) sts on last row—28 (30, 30, 32) sts. Change to larger needles and work in St st, inc 1 st each side every 4th row 3 (3, 6, 7) times,

FRONT (CHECKERBOARD DOG)

Work as for back until piece measures 2¾ (3½, 4½, 5)"/7 (9, 11, 13)cm from beg, end with a WS row.

Beg chart pat

Row 1 (RS) With MC, k6 (9, 12, 14), work row 1 of checkerboard dog chart over next 48 sts, k to end with MC. Cont in chart as established through row 48, and AT THE SAME TIME, when same length as back to armhole, shape armhole same as back. After all chart rows have been worked, cont with MC only until armhole measures 3½ (4, 4, 4½)"/9 (10, 10, 11.5)cm.

Shape neck

Next row (RS) Work first 20 (22, 24, 25) sts, join 2nd ball of yarn and bind off center 8 (10, 10, 12) sts for neck, work to end. Working both sides at once, bind off from each neck edge 3 sts once, 2 sts once, dec 1 st every other row 3 times.

CHECKERBOARD DOG

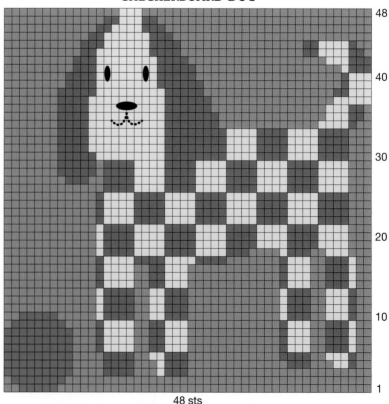

48 sts

COLOR KEY
■ Lt brown (MC)   ■ Black (B)
□ Cream (A)   ■ Red (C)

STITCH KEY
● Black satin stitch
••• Black chain stitch

every 6th row 8 (9, 8, 9) times—50 (54, 58, 64) sts. Work even until piece measures 11½ (12½, 13½, 15)"/29 (31.5, 34.5, 38)cm from beg. Bind off.

FINISHING
Block pieces to measurements. Sew right shoulder seam.

Neckband
With RS facing and MC, pick up and k 62 (67, 67, 72) sts evenly around neck edge. Work in k3, p2 rib for 4 rows. Bind off loosely in rib. Sew left shoulder and neckband seam.
Set in sleeves, sewing last 1"/2.5cm at top of sleeve to bound-off armhole sts. Sew side and sleeve seams. ■

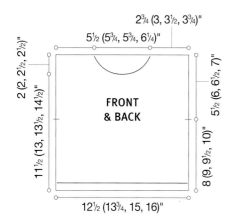

2¾ (3, 3½, 3¾)"
5½ (5¾, 5¾, 6¼)"
2 (2, 2½, 2½)"
5½ (6, 6½, 7)"
FRONT & BACK
11½ (13, 13½, 14½)"
8 (9, 9½, 10)"
12½ (13¾, 15, 16)"

11 (12, 13, 14)"
SLEEVES
11½ (12½, 13½, 15)"
6¼ (6½, 6½, 7)"

DOG WITH SCARF

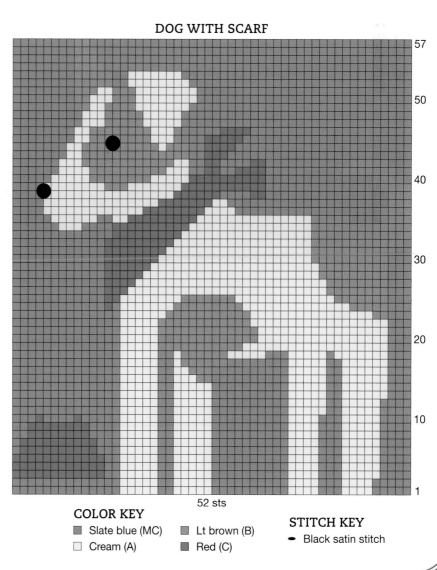

57
50
40
30
20
10
1

52 sts

COLOR KEY
- ■ Slate blue (MC)
- □ Cream (A)
- ■ Lt brown (B)
- ■ Red (C)

STITCH KEY
- ● Black satin stitch

STRIPED vest

SIZES
Sized for Child's 2, 4, 6, 8 and 10. Shown in size 6.

MEASUREMENTS
Chest 26 (28, 30, 32, 33)"/66 (71, 76, 81, 83.5)cm
Length 16 (17,18, 20, 22)"/40 (43, 45.5, 51, 56)cm

GAUGE
18 sts and 25 rows to 4"/10cm over St st using size 8 (5mm) needles.
Take time to check gauge.

STRIPE PATTERN
With A work in St st for 6"/15cm.
With B work in rev St st for 3"/7.5cm.
With C work in St st for 3"/7.5cm.
With D work in rev St st for 3"/7.5cm.
With E work in St st to end.

NOTE
When changing from St st (k on RS, p on WS) to rev St st (p on RS, k on WS), k 1 row in new color on RS.

BACK
With A, cast on 58 (64, 68, 72, 74) sts. Work in stripe pat for 11¾ (12¼, 13, 14½, 16)"/30 (31, 33, 37, 40.5)cm.

Shape armhole
Bind off 4 sts at beg of next 2 rows, 0 (2, 2, 2, 2) sts at beg of next 2 rows. Dec 1 st each side every other row 2 (1, 1, 1, 1) times—46 (50, 54, 58, 60) sts. Work even in stripe pat until armhole measures 4¼ (4¾, 5, 5½, 6)"/10.5 (12, 12.5, 14, 15.5)cm.

Shape shoulder
Bind off 12 (13, 15, 16, 16) sts at beg of next 2 rows. Place rem 22 (24, 24, 26, 28) sts on a holder for neck.

MATERIALS
Yarn ④
Any worsted weight wool yarn
- 3½oz/100g, 190yd/180m (5¼oz/150g, 290yd/270m; 5¼oz/150g, 290yd/270m; 7oz/200g, 380yd/350m; 7oz/200g, 380yd/350m) in copper (A)
- 1¾oz/50g, 100yd/90m (1¾oz/50g, 100yd/90m; 1¾oz/50g, 100yd/90m; 3½oz/100g, 190yd/180m; 5¼oz/150g, 290yd/270m) in beige (E)
- 1¾oz/50g, 100yd/90m (3½oz/100g, 190yd/180m; 3½oz/100g, 190yd/180m; 3½oz/100g, 190yd/180m; 3½oz/100g, 190yd/180m) each in teal (B), olive (C) and medium brown (D)

Needles
- One pair size 8 (5mm) needles *or size to obtain gauge*
- One size 8 (5mm) circular needle, 16"/40cm long

Notions
- Stitch markers and holders

FRONT
Work as for back until piece measures 13½ (14½, 15½, 17½, 19½)"/34 (36.5, 39, 44.5, 49.5)cm from beg, end with a WS row.

Shape neck
Next row (RS) Work 19 (20, 22, 23, 23) sts, join 2nd ball of yarn and bind off center 8 (10, 10, 12, 14) sts, work to end. Working both sides at once, bind off 3 sts from each neck edge once, 2 sts once. Dec 1 st at each neck edge every other row 2 times. Work even until same length as back. Bind off rem 12 (13, 15, 16, 16) sts each side for shoulders.

FINISHING
Block pieces to measurements. Sew shoulder seams.

Neckband
With RS facing, circular needle and D, pick up and k 64 (68, 68, 72, 76) sts evenly around neck edge. Join and work in St st (k every rnd) for 1½"/4cm. Bind off loosely.

Armhole band
With RS facing, circular needle and A, pick up and k 48 (54, 56, 60, 64) sts evenly around each armhole edge. Beg with a p row on WS, work in St st for 5 rows. Bind off knitwise. Sew side and armhole band seams. ■

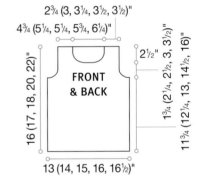

2¾ (3, 3¼, 3½, 3½)"
4¾ (5¼, 5¼, 5¾, 6¼)"
2½"
16 (17, 18, 20, 22)"
1¾ (2¼, 2½, 3, 3½)"
11¾ (12¼, 13, 14½, 16)"
FRONT & BACK
13 (14, 15, 16, 16½)"

CABLED sweater

SIZES
Sized for Child's 6 (8, 10, 12). Shown in size 6.

MEASUREMENTS
Chest 26 (29, 32, 35)"/66 (73.5, 81, 89)cm
Length 16 (17½, 19, 20½)"/40.5 (44.5, 48, 52)cm
Upper arm 12 (13, 14, 15)"/30.5 (33, 35.5, 38)cm

GAUGE
16 sts and 20 rows to 4"/10cm over seed st using larger needles.
Take time to check gauge.

K1, P1 RIB
(over an odd number of sts)
Row 1 (RS) *K1, p1; rep from * to last st, k1.
Row 2 K the knit sts and p the purl sts. Rep row 2 for k1, p1 rib.

SEED STITCH
Row 1 (RS) *K1, p1; rep from * to end.
Row 2 K the purl sts and p the knit sts. Rep row 2 for seed st.

CABLED PATTERN
(over 8 sts)
Rows 1 and 3 (RS) P1, k6, p1.
Row 2 and all WS rows K1, p6, k1.
Row 5 P1, sl 3 sts to cn and hold to back, k3, k3 from cn, p1.
Rows 7 and 9 Rep row 1.
Row 10 Rep row 2.
Rep rows 1–10 for cable pat.

BACK
With smaller needles, cast on 59 (65, 71, 77) sts. Work in k1, p1 rib for 1½"/4cm, inc 5 sts evenly spaced across last row and end with a WS row—64 (70, 76, 82) sts. Change to larger needles.

MATERIALS
Yarn ④
• 8¾oz/250g, 390yd/360m (10½oz/300g, 470yd/430m; 14oz/400g, 620yd/570m; 15¾oz/450g, 700yd/640m) of any worsted weight wool yarn in yellow

Needles
• One pair each sizes 8 and 9 (5 and 5.5mm) knitting needles *or size to obtain gauge*
• Size 8 (5mm) circular needle, 16"/40cm long

Notions
• Cable needle (cn)
• Stitch holders
• Stitch marker

Beg pats
Next row (RS) Work 6 (7, 6, 7) sts seed st, [8 sts cable pat, 3 (4, 6, 7) sts seed st] 4 times, 8 sts cable pat, 6 (7, 6, 7) sts seed st. Cont in pats as established until piece measures 10 (11, 12, 13)"/25.5 (28, 30.5, 33)cm from beg, end with a WS row.

Shape armholes
Bind off 5 sts at beg of next 2 rows—54 (60, 66, 72) sts. Work even until armhole measures 6 (6½, 7, 7½)"/15 (16.5, 17.5, 19)cm, end with a WS row.

Shape shoulders
Bind off 15 (17, 20, 22) sts at beg of next 2 rows. Place rem 24 (26, 26, 28) sts on holder for back neck.

FRONT
Work as for back until armhole measures 4 (4½, 5, 5½)"/10 (11.5, 12.5, 14) cm, end with a WS row.

Shape neck
Next row (RS) Work across first 20 (22, 25, 27) sts, place center 14 (16, 16, 18) sts on holder for front neck, join another ball of yarn, work to end. Working both sides at once, bind off from each neck edge 2 sts once, then dec 1 st each side every other row 3 times—15 (17, 20, 22) sts each side. Work even until piece measures same length as back to shoulder, end with a WS row. Bind off each side.

SLEEVES
With smaller needles, cast on 31 (33, 35, 37) sts. Work in k1, p1 rib for 1½"/4cm, inc 5 sts evenly spaced across last row and end with a WS row—36 (38, 40, 42) sts. Change to larger needles.

Beg pats
Next row (RS) Work 3 (3, 2, 2) sts seed st, [8 sts cable pat, 3 (4, 6, 7) sts seed st] twice, 8 sts cable pat, 3 (3, 2, 2) sts seed st.
Cont in pats as established until piece measures 2½"/6.5cm from beg, end with a WS row. Working inc in seed st, inc 1 st each side on next row, then every 4th row 3 (4, 4, 5) times more, every 6th row 5 (5, 6, 6) times—54 (58, 62, 66) sts. Work even until piece measures 11 (12, 13, 14)"/28 (30.5, 33, 35.5)cm from beg. Mark beg and end of last row for beg of cap. Cont to work even for 1"/2.5cm, end with a WS row.

Shape cap
Bind off 4 (4, 5, 5) sts at beg of next 8 rows. Bind off rem 22 (26, 22, 26) sts.

FINISHING
Lightly block pieces to measurements. Sew shoulder seams.

Neckband

With RS facing and circular needle,
pick up and k 62 (66, 66, 70) sts evenly
spaced around neck edge, including sts
from holders. Join and pm for beg of
rnd.

Rnd 1 *K1, p1; rep from * around.
Rep rnd 1 for k1, p1 rib for 1"/2.5cm.
Bind off all sts loosely in rib.
Set in sleeves, sewing 1"/2.5cm above
sleeve markers to bound-off armhole sts.
Sew side and sleeve seams. ■

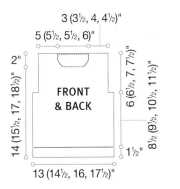

3 (3½, 4, 4½)"
5 (5½, 5½, 6)"
2"
6 (6½, 7, 7½)"

FRONT & BACK

14 (15½, 17, 18½)"

6 (6½, 7, 7½)"
8½ (9½, 10½, 11½)"
1½"

13 (14½, 16, 17½)"

12 (13, 14, 15)"
1" 1"

SLEEVES

9½ (10½, 11½, 12½)"
1½"

6 (6½, 6½, 7)"

OCTOPUS sweater

SIZES
Sized for Child's 4 (6, 8). Shown in size 4.

MEASUREMENTS
Chest 30 (33, 36)"/76 (84, 91.5)cm
Length (excluding rolled edge) 16 (17, 18)"/40.5 (43, 45.5)cm
Upper arm 13 (14, 15)"/33 (35.5, 38)cm

GAUGE
22 sts and 28 rows to 4"/10cm over St st using larger needles.
Take time to check gauge.

STRIPE PATTERN
Working in St st, *work 6 rows MC, 6 rows CC; rep from * (12 rows) for stripe pat.

BACK
With smaller needles and CC, cast on 82 (90, 100) sts. Work in St st for 8 rows. Mark beg and end of last row for end of rolled edge. Change to larger needles and MC. Cont in St st and work even until piece measures 16 (17, 18)"/40.5 (43, 45.5) cm from marked row, end with a WS row.

Shape shoulders
Bind off 26 (29, 33) sts at beg of next 2 rows. Place rem 30 (32, 34) sts on holder for back neck.

FRONT
Work as for back until piece measures 13½ (14½, 15½)"/34 (37, 39.5)cm from marked row, end with a WS row.

Shape neck
Next row (RS) K33 (36, 40), place center 16 (18, 20) sts on holder for front neck, join another ball of MC, k to end. Working both sides at once, p next row.

MATERIALS
Yarn ③
Any DK weight cotton and acrylic blend yarn
- 7oz/200g, 550yd/510m (8¾oz/250g, 680yd/630m; 10½oz/300g, 820yd/750m) in blue (MC)
- 3½oz/100g, 280yd/260m (5¼oz/150g, 410yd/380m; 5¼oz/150g, 410yd/380m) in green (CC)

Needles
- One pair each sizes 5 and 6 (3.75 and 4mm) needles
  or size to obtain gauge
- Size 5 (3.75mm) circular needle, 16"/40cm long

Dec row (RS) With first ball of yarn, k to last 3 sts, k2tog, k1, with 2nd ball of yarn, k1, ssk, k to end—32 (35, 39) sts each side. P next row. Rep last 2 rows 6 times more—26 (29, 33) sts each side. Work even until piece measures same length as back to shoulder. Bind off each side for shoulders.

SLEEVES
With smaller needles and CC, cast on 37 (39, 41) sts. Work in St st for 8 rows. Mark beg and end of last row for end of rolled edge. Change to larger needles and cont in stripe pat, AT THE SAME TIME, inc 1 st each side on next row, then every 4th row 10 (12, 14) times more, then every 6th row 6 times—71 (77, 83) sts.
Work even until piece measures 12 (13½, 14½)"/30.5 (34, 37)cm from marked row, end with a WS row. Bind off.

FINISHING
Block pieces to measurements. Duplicate st octopus on center of front beg 40 (44, 48) rows from rolled edge. Using MC, embroider French knots eyes and stem stitch smile. Sew shoulder seams.

Neckband
With RS facing, circular needle and CC, pick up and k 74 (78, 82) sts evenly spaced around neck edge including sts on holders. Join and k 8 rnds. Bind off all sts loosely knitwise.

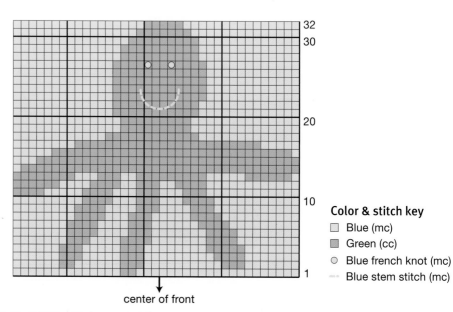

center of front

Color & stitch key
- ☐ Blue (mc)
- ▨ Green (cc)
- ◯ Blue french knot (mc)
- ˗˗ Blue stem stitch (mc)

Place markers 6½ (7, 7½)"/16.5 (17.5, 19)cm down from shoulders on back and front. Sew sleeves to armholes between markers. Sew side and sleeve seams. ■

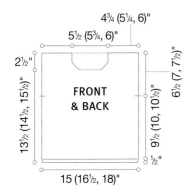

FRONT & BACK

5½ (5¾, 6)"

4¾ (5¼, 6)"

2½"

13½ (14½, 15½)"

9½ (10, 10½)"

6½ (7, 7½)"

½"

15 (16½, 18)"

13 (14, 15)"

SLEEVES

12 (13½, 14½)"

½"

6¾ (7, 7½)"

Nick Norwood

SAILOR top

SIZES
Sized for Child's 1, 2, 4, and 6. Shown in size 1.

MEASUREMENTS
Chest 24 (26, 28, 30)"/61 (66, 71, 76)cm
Length 11 (12½, 14, 15)"/28 (31.5, 35.5, 38)cm
Upper arm 11 (11½, 12½, 13)"/28 (29, 32, 33)cm

GAUGE
18 sts and 26 rows to 4"/10cm over St st using size 8 (5mm) needles.
Take time to check gauge.

BACK
With smaller needles and MC, cast on 54 (58, 64, 68) sts. Work in St st for 4 rows.
Next (picot) row (RS) K1, *yo, k2tog; rep from *, end k1. P 1 row. Change to larger needles and cont in St st until piece measures 2"/5cm above picot row. Change to CC and cont in St st for 6 rows. Change to MC and cont in St st until piece measures 11 (12½, 14, 15)"/28 (31.5, 35.5, 38)cm above picot row, end with a WS row.
Next row (RS) K18 (19, 22, 24) and place sts on a holder for right back shoulder, bind off center 18 (20, 20, 20) sts for back neck, k to end and place rem 18 (19, 22, 24) sts on a holder for left back shoulder.

FRONT
Work as for back until piece measures 6½ (8, 9, 10)"/16.5 (20.5, 23, 25.5)cm above picot row, end with a WS row.

Shape placket
Next row (RS) K29 (31, 34, 36), join 2nd ball of MC and cast on 4 sts, k to end—29 (31, 34, 36) sts each side. Work both sides at once with separate balls of yarn as foll:
Next row (WS) P to last 4 sts of first half, k4; on 2nd half, k4, p to end.
Next row K all sts on both sides.
Rep last 2 rows until placket measures 1¼"/3cm, end with a WS row.
Next (buttonhole) row (RS) K sts on first side; 2nd side, k2, yo, k2tog, k to end. Work even for 1¼"/3cm, end with a WS row. Rep buttonhole row. Work even until placket measures 3"/7.5cm.

Shape neck
Bind off from each neck edge 6 (7, 7, 7) sts once, 3 sts once, 2 sts once. Work even, if necessary, on rem 18 (19, 22, 24) sts until same length as back. Place sts each side on holders.

Join shoulders
With WS of pieces facing each other (front of garment facing you), sl sts of left front shoulder to one dpn and sts of left back shoulder to 2nd dpn. Work

3-needle bind-off as foll: With a 3rd dpn, k first st on front needle tog with first st on back needle, *k next st from front and back needles tog, pass the first st over the 2nd st to bind off; rep from * until all sts are bound-off. Join right shoulders in same way.

SLEEVES
Place markers on front and back 5½ (5¾, 6¼, 6½)"/14 (14.5, 16, 16.5)cm down from shoulder seams. With RS facing, larger needle and MC, pick up and k 50 (52, 56, 58) sts evenly between markers. Beg with a WS row, work in St st for 3 rows. Dec 1 st each side on next row, then rep dec every 8th row 0 (3, 3, 0) times, every 6th row 8 (6, 7, 11) times, AT THE SAME TIME, when piece measures 6 (7½, 8½, 9)"/15.5 (19, 21.5, 23)cm from pick up row, change to CC and work 6 rows, then change to MC to end of piece. Work even on rem 32 (32, 34, 34) sts until sleeve measures 9 (10½, 11½, 12)"/23 (26.5, 29, 30.5)cm from pick up row, end with a RS row. Change to smaller needles and purl 1 row. Work picot row as for back. Beg with a WS row, work in St st for 4 rows. Bind off.

FINISHING
Sew side and sleeve seams. Fold hems at picot row to WS and sew in place. Lap buttonhole placket over button placket and sew in place along center bound-off sts. Sew on buttons opposite buttonholes.

Left collar
With larger needles and CC, cast on 18 sts. Work in garter st for 5 rows.
Next row (WS) K3, p to last 3 sts, k3. Cont as established, keeping first and last 3 sts in garter st and rem sts in St st, until piece measures 2"/5cm from beg, end with a RS row.

MATERIALS
Yarn (4)
Any worsted weight cotton yarn
• 5¼oz/150g, 270yd/250m (7oz/200g, 360yd/330m; 8¾/250g, 450yd/420m; 8¾oz/250g, 450yd/420m) in blue (MC)
• 1¾oz/50g, 90yd/82m in white (CC)

Needles
• One pair each sizes 7 and 8 (4.5 and 5mm) needles
or size to obtain gauge
• Three size 8 (5mm) double-pointed needles (dpns) for joining shoulders

Notions
• Stitch holders and markers
• Two ½"/13mm buttons

Shape neck

Next row (WS) Bind off 3 sts, work to end. Cont to bind off from neck edge 2 sts once more—13 sts. Work even in pat, with garter st at outside edge only, until piece measures 3½"/9cm from beg, end with a WS row. Place sts on a holder.

Right collar

Work to correspond to left collar, reversing all shaping. Leave sts on needle, do not place on a holder.

Join collar

Slip left collar sts to needle with right collar sts.

Next row (RS) Work 13 sts from left collar, cast on 18 (20, 20, 20) sts, work 13 sts from right collar—44 (46, 46, 46) sts. Keeping first and last 3 sts in garter and rem sts in St st, work even for 3½"/9cm, end with a RS row. Work 4 rows in garter st, then bind off. Place collar, RS up over sweater, aligning neck edges and sew in place. ■

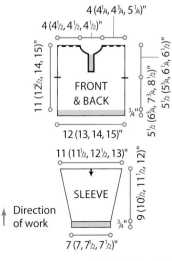

4 (4¼, 4¾, 5¼)"

4 (4½, 4½, 4½)"

11 (12½, 14, 15)"

FRONT & BACK

5½ (6¾, 7¾, 8½)"

5½ (5¾, 6¼, 6½)"

¾"

12 (13, 14, 15)"

11 (11½, 12½, 13)"

9 (10½, 11½, 12)"

SLEEVE

↑ Direction of work

¾"

7 (7, 7½, 7½)"

BANDED vest

SIZES
Sized for Child's 4 (6, 8, 10). Shown in size 6.

MEASUREMENTS
Chest 30 (32, 34, 36)"/76 (81, 86.5, 91.5)cm
Length 16 (17, 18, 19)"/40.5 (43, 45.5, 48)cm

GAUGE
19 sts and 25 rows to 4"/10cm over St st using size 7 (4.5mm) needles.
Take time to check gauge.

CABLE RIB
(multiple of 4 sts plus 2)
Row 1 (WS) P1, *p3, k1; rep from *, end p1.
Row 2 K1, *p1, sl next st to cn and hold to *back*, k1, k1 from cn, k1; rep from *, end k1.
Row 3 Rep row 1.
Row 4 K1, *p1, k1, sl next st to cn and hold to *front*, k1, k1 from cn; rep from *, end k1.
Rep rows 1–4 for cable rib.

COLOR BAND
(multiple of 2 sts plus 1)
Row 1 (WS) With MC, p1, *with A, p1, with MC, p1; rep from * to end.
Row 2 With A, k.
Row 3 With A, p.
Rows 4 and 5 With B, k.
Row 6 With C, k1, *sl 1 wyib, k1; rep from * to end.
Row 7 With C, k1, *sl 1 wyif, k1; rep from * to end.
Rows 8 and 9 Rep row 4.
Row 10 With A, k2, *sl 1 wyib, k1; rep from *, end k1.
Row 11 With A, p2, *sl 1 wyif, p1; rep from *, end p1.
Work rows 1–11 for color band.

MATERIALS
Yarn (4)
Any worsted weight wool yarn
- 7oz/200g, 340yd/320m (7oz/200g, 340yd/320m; 10½oz/600g, 500yd/460m; 10½oz/600g, 500yd/460m;) in teal (MC)
- 3½oz/100g, 170yd/160m each in green (A), light blue (B) and light yellow (C)

Needles
- One pair size 7 (4.5mm) knitting needles *or size to obtain gauge*

Notions
- Cable needle (cn)

BACK
With A, cast on 74 (78, 82, 86) sts. Change to MC and work in cable rib for 2"/5cm, end with a RS row. P next row, dec 1 st—73 (77, 81, 85) sts.
Cont in St st until piece measures 9 (9½, 10, 10½)"/23 (24, 25.5, 26.5)cm from beg, ending with a WS row.

Shape armholes
Bind off 5 sts at beg of next 2 rows, then 2 sts at beg of next 2 rows.
Dec row (RS) K1, ssk, k to last 3 sts, k2tog, k1. P next row.
Rep last 2 rows 3 times more—51 (55, 59, 63) sts.
Work even until armhole measures 6½ (7, 7½, 8)"/16.5 (17.5, 19, 20.5)cm, ending with a WS row.

Shape neck
Next row (RS) K14 (15, 17, 18) sts, join another ball of MC and bind off center 23 (25, 25, 27) sts, k to end.
Working both sides at once, dec 1 st at each neck edge every row once. Work even on 13 (14, 16, 17) sts each side until armhole measures 7 (7½, 8, 8½)"/17.5 (19, 20.5, 21.5)cm. Bind off.

FRONT
Work as for back until piece measures 8 (8½, 9, 9½)"/20.5 (21.5, 23, 24)cm from beg, end with a RS row. Work rows 1–11 of color band, AT THE SAME TIME, when piece measures same length as back to armhole, shape armholes same as back. When color band is completed, cont with MC only and St st until armhole measures 2½ (3, 3, 3)"/6.5 (7.5, 7.5, 7.5)cm, ending with a WS row.

Shape neck
Next row (RS) K22 (24, 26, 28) sts, k2tog, k1, join another ball of MC and bind off center st, k1, ssk, k to end. Working both sides at once, p next row.
Dec row (RS) With first ball of yarn, k to last 3 sts, k2tog, k1, with 2nd ball of yarn, k1, ssk k to end. P next row.
Rep last 2 rows 10 (11, 11, 12) times more—13 (14, 16, 17) sts each side. Work even until piece measures same length as back to shoulder. Bind off.

FINISHING
Block pieces to measurements. Sew left shoulder seam.

Neck edging
With RS facing and A, pick up and k 88 (90, 98, 106) sts evenly spaced along neck edge. Bind off in rib. Sew right shoulder seam.

Armhole edging
With RS facing and MC, pick up and k 81 (87, 93, 97) sts evenly spaced along armhole edge. Bind off in rib. Sew side seams. ■

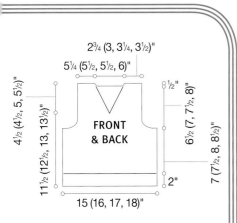

2¾ (3, 3¼, 3½)"

5¼ (5½, 5½, 6)"

½"

4½ (4½, 5, 5½)"

FRONT & BACK

6½ (7, 7½, 8)"

11½ (12½, 13, 13½)"

2"

7 (7½, 8, 8½)"

15 (16, 17, 18)"

Rose Callahan

SNAKE sweater

SIZES
Sized for Child's 4, 6, 8, 10. Shown in size 6.

MEASUREMENTS
Chest (closed) 28 (30, 32, 35)"/71 (76, 81, 89)cm
Length 18¼ (19½, 21, 22½)"/46.5 (49.5, 53.5, 57)cm
Upper arm 11 (11½, 12¾, 13½)"/28 (29, 32.5, 34.5)cm

GAUGE
19 sts and 28 rows to 4"/10cm over St st using size 8 (5mm) needles.
Take time to check gauge.

K3, P3 RIB
(multiple of 6 sts plus 3)
Row 1 (RS) K3, *p3, k3; rep from * to end.
Row 2 P3, *k3, p3; rep from * to end.
Rep rows 1 and 2 for k3, p3 rib.

STRIPE PATTERN
Working in St st, *work 6 rows A, 2 rows B; rep from * (8 rows) for stripe pat.

BACK
With MC, cast on 75 (81, 87, 93) sts. Work in k3, p3 rib for 2¼ (2¾, 2¾, 3)"/5.5 (7, 7, 7.5)cm, end with a WS row.
Next (dec) row (RS) K across, dec 8 (10, 10, 10) sts evenly spaced—67 (71, 77, 83) sts.
Beg with a p row, cont in St st until piece measures 12 (13, 14, 15)"/30.5 (33, 35.5, 38)cm from beg, end with a WS row.

Shape raglan armholes
Bind off 4 (4, 5, 5) sts at beg of next 2 rows.
Dec row (RS) K2, k2tog, work to last 4 sts, ssk, k2. P next row.

MATERIALS
Yarn (4)
Any worsted weight wool yarn
• 14oz/400g, 670yd/630m (14oz/400g, 670yd/630m; 17½oz/500g, 830yd/760m; 21oz/600g, 1000yd/920m) in cream (MC)
• 3½oz/100g, 170yd/160m each in green (A) and light yellow (B)
• Small amount in dark red (C)

Needles
• One pair size 8 (5mm) needles *or size to obtain gauge*
• Size 8 (5mm) circular needle, 24"/60cm long

Notions
• Stitch holders
• Stitch markers
• Six ¾"/19mm buttons
• Two ¼"/10mm yellow acrylic faceted beads
• Three ¾"/19mm gold jingle bells
• Three ½"/18mm jingle bells
• A small package of quilt batting
• Small amount of polyester fiberfill
• Sewing thread

Rep last 2 rows 18 (19, 21, 23) times more. Place rem 21 (23, 23, 25) sts on holder for back neck.

LEFT FRONT
With MC, cast on 39 (39, 45, 45) sts. Work in k3, p3 rib for 2¼ (2¾, 2¾, 3)"/5.5 (7, 7, 7.5)cm, end with a WS row.
Next (dec) row (RS) K across, dec 6 (4, 7, 4) sts evenly spaced—33 (35, 38, 41) sts. Beg with a p row, cont in St st until piece measures same length as back to underarm, end with a WS row.

Shape raglan armhole and neck
Bind off 4 (4, 5, 5) sts, k to last 2 sts, k2tog (neck edge). Cont to shape raglan armhole same as back by working k2,

k2tog at beg of every RS row. AT THE SAME TIME, cont to dec 1 st at neck edge every 6th row 7 (8, 8, 9) times more. When all shaping has been completed, place rem 3 sts on holder for left front neck.

RIGHT FRONT
Work same as left front, reversing all shaping by binding off for armhole on a WS row, and working raglan decs at end of RS rows by knitting to last 4 sts, k2tog, k2. Work neck decs at beg of every 6th row.

SLEEVES
With MC, cast on 33 (39, 39, 39) sts. Cont in k3, p3 rib for 4½ (5, 5, 5½)"/11.5 (12.5, 12.5, 14)cm, end with a WS row.
Cont in St st. Inc 1 st each side on next row, then every 4th row 3 (0, 1, 5) times more, every 6th row 6 (3, 9, 7) times, every 8th row 0 (4, 0, 0) times—53 (55, 61, 65) sts.
Work even until piece measures 12½ (13½, 14½, 16½)"/31.5 (34, 37, 42)cm from beg, end with a WS row.

Shape raglan cap
Work as for back. Place rem 7 sts on holder.

POCKETS (MAKE 2)
With MC, cast on 21 sts. Work in St st for 3 (3, 3½, 3½)"/7.5 (7.5, 9, 9)cm, end with a WS row. Cont in k3, p3 rib for ¾ (¾, ¾, 1)"/2 (2, 2, 2.5)cm. Bind off in rib.

FINISHING
Block pieces to measurements. Sew each pocket to front, so lower edge is ½ (½, ¾, 1)"/1.5 (1.5, 2, 2.5)cm from top of ribbing and centered side to side. Join raglan seams. Sew side and sleeve seams, reversing seams over last 2 (2½, 2½,

SNAKE sweater

2½")/5 (6.5, 6.5, 6.5)cm of sleeves for turnback.

Place markers for 5 button-holes on left front, with the first ½"/1.5cm from lower edge, the 2nd 1¾"/4.5cm from lower edge, the last at beg of neck shaping and 2 evenly spaced between; 6th button is used for decorative purposes only and does not have a corresponding buttonhole.

Front band

With RS facing, circular needle and MC, pick up and k 95 (103, 112, 117) sts evenly spaced along right front edge, k 3 sts from right front holder, 7 sts from right sleeve holder, 21 (23, 23, 25) sts from back neck holder, 7 sts from left sleeve holder, 3 sts from left front holder, then pick up and k 95 (103, 112, 117) sts along left front edge—231 (249, 267, 279) sts. Do not join. Beg with row 2, and working back and forth, cont in k3, p3 rib for 1 row.

Next (buttonhole) row (RS)
*Work in rib to marker, bind off next 2 sts; rep from * 5 times more, work to end.

Next row Work in rib, casting on 2 sts over bound-off sts. Work in rib for 1 row. Bind off loosely in rib. Sew on buttons. On right front band, sew 6th button above 5th (top) button, spacing it the same as the 4th and 5th buttons.

SNAKE

Rattle tail

With B, cast on 5 sts, leaving a long tail for sewing.
***Next (inc) row (RS)** [K in front and back of next st] 5 times—10 sts. Beg with a p row, cont in St st for ¾"/2cm, end with a RS row.

Next (dec) row (WS) [P2tog] 5 times—5 sts.
Rep from * twice more—5 sts.

Body

Change to A and stripe pat.
Next (inc) row K1, M1, k to last st, M1, k1—7 sts. Beg with a p row, work in St st for 9 rows.
Rep last 10 rows 8 times more—23 sts. Mark last row. Work even until piece measures 12"/30.5cm above marked row, end with 2 rows of B. Change to A.

Head

Next (inc) row (RS) K3, *k into front and back of next st, k1; rep from * to end—33 sts. Beg with a p row, cont in St st for 1"/2.5cm.

Shape mouth

Dec row 1 (RS) K9, sl 2 sts tog, k1, pass 2 sl sts over k st, k to last 12 sts, sl 2 sts tog, k1, pass 2 sl sts over k st, k9—29 sts. P next row.
Dec row 2 (RS) K8, sl 2 sts tog, k1, pass 2 sl sts over k st, k to last 11 sts, sl 2 sts tog, k1, pass 2 sl sts over k st, k8—25 sts. P next row.
Dec row 3 (RS) K7, sl 2 sts tog, k1, pass 2 sl sts over k st, k to last 10 sts, sl 2 sts tog, k1, pass 2 sl sts over k st, k7—21 sts. P next row.
Dec row 4 (RS) K6, sl 2 sts tog, k1, pass 2 sl sts over k st, k to last 9 sts, sl 2 sts tog, k1, pass 2 sl sts over k st, k6—17 sts. P next row.
Dec row 5 (RS) K5, sl 2 sts tog, k1, pass 2 sl sts over k st, k 1, sl 2 sts tog, k1, pass 2 sl sts over k st, k5—13 sts. P next row.
Dec row 6 (RS) K1, [k2tog] twice, SK2P, [k2tog] twice, k1—7 sts. P next row.
Dec row 7 (RS) K2 tog, k3tog, k2tog—3 sts.
Dec row 8 (WS) P3tog—1 st. Fasten off last st.

Tongue

With C, cast on 8 sts. Bind off leaving a long tail for sewing.

FINISHING

Using thread doubled in sewing needle, sew on bead eyes. Sew end of tongue under tip of mouth using yarn tail. Stuff the snake (see How-To).
Referring to photo, drape snake around neck, then pin in place, forming lower half of body in gentle "S" curves and leaving tongue and rattle tail free. Sew snake in place from WS using MC. Tack tongue in place on sweater using C. ■

Here's a closeup look at finishing the snake.

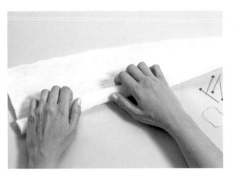

Roll it

1 Cut the batting approximately 22"/56cm long and 12"/30.5cm at the widest point, tapering it along the length to match the shape of the snake's body. Roll the batting lengthwise into a tight roll.

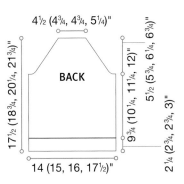

BACK

4½ (4¾, 4¾, 5¼)"

17½ (18¾, 20¼, 21¾)"

9¾ (10¼, 11¼, 12)"

5½ (5¾, 6¼, 6¾)"

2¼ (2¾, 2¾, 3)"

14 (15, 16, 17½)"

Baste it

2 Pin the rolled batting in place every few inches. With sewing needle and thread, baste the roll together, removing the pins as you go.

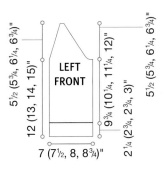

LEFT FRONT

5½ (5¾, 6¼, 6¾)"

5½ (5¾, 6¼, 6¾)"

12 (13, 14, 15)"

9¾ (10¼, 11¼, 12)"

2¼ (2¾, 2¾, 3)"

7 (7½, 8, 8¾)"

Close it

3 Wrap the knitted snake around the roll, with the wider section of the roll at the neck, just under the head, ending about 10"/25.5cm before the end of the tail. Pin the edges of the fabric together. Stuff the head with fiberfill.

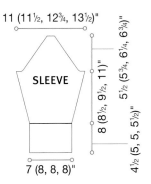

SLEEVE

11 (11½, 12¾, 13½)"

8 (8½, 9½, 11)"

5½ (5¾, 6¼, 6¾)"

4½ (5, 5, 5½)"

7 (8, 8, 8)"

Finish it

4 Sew the back seam of the fabric where the batting and fiberfill are placed, being sure to match the stripes. The rest of the tail can remain unsewn until you attach it to the sweater. Insert the bells into the tail end and sew the tail together.

DOG
sweater & hat

SIZES
Sized for Child's 2, 4 and 6. Shown in size 2.

MEASUREMENTS
Sweater
Chest 26½ (28, 30)"/67 (71, 76)cm
Length 15¼ (16¼, 17¼)"/38.5 (41, 44)cm
Upper arm 11½ (12½, 13)"/29 (31.5, 33)cm

Hat
Circumference 16 (17, 18)"/40.5(43, 45.5)cm
Length 7½(8, 8½")/19 (20.5, 21.5)cm

GAUGE
18 sts and 26 rows to 4"/10cm over St st using larger needles.
Take time to check gauge.

STRIPE PATTERN
Row 1 (RS) With A, knit.
Row 2 With A, purl.
Rows 3 and 4 With B, rep rows 1 and 2. Rep rows 1–4 for stripe pat.

NOTE
When changing colors, twist yarns on WS to prevent holes in work. Use a separate bobbin for each color section. Do not carry yarn across back of work.

Sweater
BACK
With larger needles and B, cast on 60 (64, 68) sts. Work in St st for 8 rows. Work in stripe pat until piece measures 15¼ (16¼, 17¼)"/38.5 (41, 44)cm from beg, end with RS row.
Next row (WS) Bind off 18 (19, 20) sts for right shoulder, p until there are 24

MATERIALS
Yarn ④
Any worsted weight wool yarn
• 8¾oz/250g, 390yd/360m (10½oz/300g, 470yd/430m; 12¼oz/350g, 540yd/500m) in ecru (A) and brown (B)
• 1¾oz/50g, 77yd/70m in red (C)

Needles
• One pair each sizes 5 and 7 (3.75 and 4.5mm) needles
or size to obtain gauge

Notions
• One size F/5 (3.75mm) crochet hook
• Stitch holder
• Bobbins for intarsia knitting
• Polyester stuffing
• 2 white 4-holed ½"/13mm buttons
• Embroidery needle and black thread

(26, 28) sts on needle and place them on a holder, bind off rem 18 (19, 20) sts for left shoulder.

FRONT
Work same as for back until piece measures 5½(6, 7)"/14 (15, 16.5)cm from beg, end with a WS row.

Beg chart 1
Next row (RS) Work 17 (19, 21) sts in stripe pat as established, work 26 sts of chart 1, join 2nd ball of stripe color and work to end.
Cont in stripe and chart pat as established until 13 rows of chart are complete. Work in stripe pat over all sts until piece measures 12¾(13¾, 14¾)"/32 (35, 37.5)cm from beg, end with a WS row.

Shape neck
Next row (RS) K24 (25, 26) join 2nd ball of yarn and bind off center 12 (14,

16) sts, k to end. Working both sides at once, bind off 2 sts at each neck edge twice, then dec 1 st at neck edge every other row twice—18 (19, 20) sts rem for each shoulder. Work even until piece measures same as back. Bind off.

SLEEVES
With larger needles and B, cast on 30 (32, 32) sts. Work in St st for 8 rows. Join A and work row 1 of stripe pat, inc 1 st each side—32 (34, 34) sts. Cont in stripe pat, inc 1 st each side every 6th row 10 (11, 12) times more—52 (56, 58) sts. Work even until piece measures 13 (14, 15)"/33 (35.5, 38)cm from beg. Bind off.

FINISHING
Block pieces to measurements. Sew left shoulder seam.

Neckband
With RS facing, smaller needles and B, beg at left shoulder, pick up and k 44 (46, 48) sts evenly along front neck, work in k1, p1 rib across 24 (26, 28) sts from back neck holder—68 (72, 76) sts. Work in k1, p1 rib for 5 rows more. Work in St st for 1"/2.5cm. Bind off loosely. Sew right shoulder and neckband seam. Place markers 5¾ (6¼, 6½)"/14.5 (16, 16.5)cm down from shoulder seams on front and back. Sew top of sleeve to front and back between markers. Sew side and sleeve seams.

Dog pocket
With larger needles and A, cast on 10 sts. Working in garter st (k every row), inc 1 st each side every other row 4 times—18 sts. Work in garter st until piece measures 1½"/4cm from beg, end with WS row.

DOG sweater & hat

Beg chart 2
Work 18 sts of chart 2. Cont in chart pat as established through row 28. Bind off.

Eyes
With black thread attach buttons as indicated on chart 2 in "X" formation.

Nose
With crochet hook and B, chain 10, form spiral and sew in place using photo as guide.

Ears (make 2)
With larger needles and B, cast on 4 sts. Work in St st and inc 1 st each side every other row 3 times—10 sts. Work 6 rows even.

Next (dec) row (RS) Ssk, k to last 2 sts, k2tog—8 sts. P 1 row.
Rep dec row once more—6 sts. Bind off. With crochet hook and B work slip st around curve of ear. Cut yarn, leaving long tail.
Place pocket using photo as guide. With crochet hook and B, attach to front with a slip st around curve of face, leaving top of pocket open. Attach ears to top of face.

Hat
With larger needles and B, cast on 72 (76, 81) sts. Work in St st for 8 rows. Join A and work in stripe pat until piece measures 6¼ (6¾, 7)"/16 (17, 18)cm from beg, end with a WS row.
Next (dec) row (RS) [K6 (6, 7), k2tog] * 9 times, k0 (4, 0). P 1 row.
Cont to dec 9 sts in this way on every RS row, working 1 less st before each k2tog—36 (40, 36) sts.
Next row (WS) Purl, dec 0 (4, 0) sts evenly across row.
Next (dec) row (RS) K2tog across—18 sts. Cut yarn, leaving tail. Draw through rem sts, tack tightly and sew seam.

Dog bone (make 2)
With larger needles and bobbin of C, cast on 3 sts. With 2nd bobbin of C, cast on 3 sts.
Next row (WS) With 2nd bobbin, p3, with first bobbin, p3.
Next (inc) row With first bobbin, [K1, M1] twice, k1, with 2nd bobbin work same as for first bobbin—5 sts each side.
Next (joining) row P5, cast on 1 st, cont with same bobbin, p5—11 sts. Cut bobbin no longer in use.

Next (inc) row (RS) K1, M1, k to last st, M1, k1—13 sts. Work 3 rows even.
Next (dec) row (RS) Ssk, k to last 2 sts, k2tog—11 sts. P 1 row. Rep last 2 rows twice more—7 sts. Work 10 rows even.
Next (inc) row (RS) K1, M1, k to last st, M1, k1—9 sts. P 1 row. Rep last 2 rows twice more—13 sts. Work 2 rows even.
Next (dec) row (RS) Ssk, k to last 2 sts, k2tog—11 sts.
Next row P5, bind off 1 st, p to end.
Next (dec) row *Ssk, k1, k2tog, join 2nd bobbin; rep from *—3 sts each side. Bind off both sides.

FINISHING
With RS tog, sew 2 bone pieces tog around edges, leaving opening for stuffing. Turn RS out, stuff lightly with polyester stuffing and sew closed. Attach tightly to center top of hat. ■

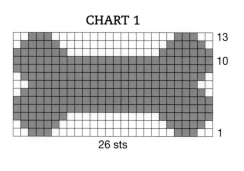

CHART 1

26 sts

COLOR KEY
☐ stripe as established
☐ Ecru (A)
▨ Brown (B)
▨ Red (C)
⊠ eye placement
❙ ear placement

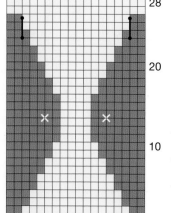

CHART 2

18 sts

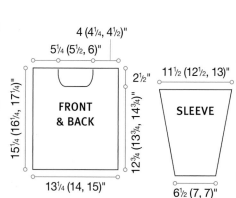

4 (4¼, 4½)"
5¼ (5½, 6)"
11½ (12½, 13)"
2½"
15¼ (16¼, 17¼)"
12¾ (13¾, 14¾)"
FRONT & BACK
13¼ (14, 15)"
SLEEVE
13 (14, 15)"
6½ (7, 7)"